RAND NATIONAL DEFENSE RESEARCH INSTITUTE

United States Service Academy Admissions

Selecting for Success at the Air Force Academy and as an Officer

Chaitra M. Hardison, Susan Burkhauser, Lawrence M. Hanser

Prepared for the Office of the Under Secretary of Defense

For more information on this publication, visit www.rand.org/t/RR744

Library of Congress Cataloging-in-Publication Data
is available for this publication.

ISBN: 978-0-8330-9182-6

Published by the RAND Corporation, Santa Monica, Calif.
© Copyright 2016 RAND Corporation
RAND® is a registered trademark.

Cover Image: DoD photo by Mike Kaplan, U.S. Air Force/Released

Support RAND
Make a tax-deductible charitable contribution at
www.rand.org/giving/contribute

www.rand.org

Preface

RAND was asked by the Office of the Under Secretary of Defense (Personnel and Readiness) to examine admission standards at the military academies to see whether the academies were enrolling not only individuals who would be successful in graduating from the academies, but also those who would be successful officers in their respective service. This report focuses on admissions to the United States Air Force Academy. A companion report (Hanser and Oguz, 2015) focuses on admissions to the U.S. Military Academy at West Point. The U.S. Naval Academy declined to participate.

These findings offer insights about legacy policies and processes that can inform future improvements to the selection process. The research reported here should be of interest to Air Force and Department of Defense senior leaders responsible for officer accession policies, including but not limited to those involved in Reserve Officer Training School, Officer Training School, and military academy accessions.

This research was sponsored by the Director of Accession Policy in the Office of the Under Secretary of Defense for Personnel and Readiness and conducted within the Forces and Resources Policy Center of the RAND National Defense Research Institute, a federally funded research and development center sponsored by the Office of the Secretary of Defense, the Joint Staff, the Unified Combatant Commands, the Navy, the Marine Corps, the defense agencies, and the defense Intelligence Community.

For more information on the RAND Forces and Resources Policy Center, see http://www.rand.org/nsrd/ndri/centers/frp.html or contact the director (contact information is provided on the web page).

Contents

Figures

Tables

Summary

United States Air Force Academy (USAFA) admissions are partly determined based on scores calculated as a weighted combination of three elements: academic composite, leadership composite, and selection panel score. This selection formula (called the selection composite) has been in place for decades, and the result has always been a class of students that is highly respected both within the Air Force and in the educational community. Nevertheless, it is still important to ask: "Can the formula be improved?"

We begin to address that question in this report through a quantitative examination of how well the elements in the formula above predict outcomes that matter to the U.S. Air Force (USAF). More specifically, we explored relationships between the following admissions factors:

- SAT/ACT composite scores
- high school (HS) rank divided by class size (hereafter referred to simply as HS rank)
- selection composite score
- leadership composite score
- academic composite score
- selection panel score

and the following USAFA and officer outcomes:

- grade point average (GPA)
- failure to graduate for academic reasons

- failure to graduate because of a desire for a career change
- military performance average (MPA)
- overall performance average (OPA)
- promotion to O-4, O-5, and O-6.

The methodology we used to explore those relationships applied statistical regression techniques and followed a predictive validation design, in which data collected on people applying to an organization are used to predict important organizational outcomes after they have joined the organization. Our data included records on the nearly 35,000 cadets who attended USAFA from 1980 to 2011 from three Air Force data sources: USAFA registrar admissions records, USAFA cadet records, and Air Force personnel records.

Although there are other factors involved in USAFA admissions process, the study scope was narrowed to include only those factors that can be impacted by USAFA policy decisions. For example, congressional nominations are one factor in the admissions process; however, nominations are not a policy lever under USAFA's control. The study analyses were also further limited to only those data that have been retained in archival data records at USAFA and in the Air Force.

Findings

The analyses show that all but one of the existing admissions factors are useful in predicting outcomes at USAFA. SAT, academic composite, leadership composite, and selection composite are significant predictors of failure to graduate for academic reasons, graduation versus choosing a career change, GPA, MPA, and OPA. HS rank was also a significant predictor of graduating versus failing for academic reasons, GPA, MPA, and OPA, but not for predicting graduating versus choosing a career change. The one admissions factor that does not appear to be working as intended is selection panel score. In the overwhelming majority of the analyses it was significant, but in the wrong direction. Higher scores were associated with a lower likelihood of success in many of the outcomes.

Our analyses also showed some interesting differences depending on which outcome was predicted. We found that the admissions factors, in general, do a much better job of predicting GPA and OPA than they do of predicting MPA. Similarly, they generally do a better job of predicting graduation versus failure for academic reasons than they do of predicting graduation versus choosing a career change. In addition, a comparison of multiple statistical models suggests that the ideal weights for each of the admissions factors would depend on the outcome being predicted. For example, for predicting failure for academic reasons, the current weights used by USAFA in computing the selection composite could be improved by weighting academic composite more heavily relative to leadership composite and excluding selection panel score entirely. In contrast, for predicting graduating versus choosing a career change, the results suggest weighting leadership composite only slightly less than the academic composite. And, lastly, academic composite should be weighted twice that of leadership composite for predicting MPA and nine times that of the leadership composite for predicting OPA and GPA.

Lastly, for predicting promotions to O-4, O-5, and O-6, we found that USAFA outcomes (GPA, MPA, and OPA) were much better predictors than the admissions factors, and MPA was a slightly better predictor than USAFA GPA.

Recommendations

Based on the results of this work, we recommend that Air Force and USAFA leadership consider three changes.

Adjust the selection composite formula. The management of the selection panel, the scoring, and the weighting of the scores are all policy levers that can be used to shape admissions to better achieve desired outcomes. The selection algorithm can and should be adjusted to best achieve these objectives. From our examination of USAFA student data and officer promotions data, we found evidence that supports the use of the current selection composite; however, we also found evidence that that the formula for this measure could be improved.

In particular, we saw repeated evidence that the use of the selection panel score in the selection composite was not helping to select the best candidates; in fact, it was hindering it. Based on this, we recommend removing the selection panel score from the selection composite formula. USAFA may instead want to consider using the selection panel score solely to screen out people that the selection panel identifies as problematic. However, because the validity of the selection panel score for use as a screening-out tool has not been confirmed, a closer examination of its validity for that use would be needed.

Although the results consistently suggested that a combination of just leadership and academic composites would be an improvement over USAFA's current selection formula, the recommended weights for combining the two composites varied noticeably across the different outcomes we predicted. As a result, no single solution exists for how best to combine the information into a single admissions formula. Nevertheless, we recommend adopting a solution that takes all of the results into consideration, and we discuss a few methods for doing so.

Collect additional information on applicants. A wide variety of measures (including personality tests, situational judgment tests, critical thinking performance tasks, and writing tests) have been identified as useful tools for predicting performance in workplace settings. It would be useful to explore whether any of these measures could add value to the USAFA selection process as well. Unfortunately, scores on these types of tests were not available in the archival data used in this study. To make such data available for future studies, we strongly encourage the Air Force to administer a variety of new measures (such as those listed above) for research purposes and—as later outcome data become available—conduct analyses similar to those presented here to identify promising additions to the selection process.

Improve data retention and maintenance. We strongly recommend that studies examining predictive validity be undertaken periodically to verify that a selection system is working as intended. However, to do so requires a rich source of longitudinal data that is well documented and maintained over time. A main finding of our study was that there is a need for increased data retention and better maintenance of USAFA's archival data sources. That data should contain scores on all possible measures taken at the time of application to the institution, should include data on people who are not admitted to USAFA, and should track cadet and officer performance over time. We also would recommend that the Air Force consider developing a method for capturing systematic performance evaluations on its officers at various points in their careers for research purposes only. If the Air Force hopes to conduct a study such as this one again in the future, it should ensure that the data being collected and retained today are maintained in such a way that they can provide data driven recommendations for policy changes in the future.

Acknowledgments

We would first like to thank our project sponsors within the Office of the Secretary of Defense, including the late Bill Carr, former Deputy Under Secretary for Military Personnel Policy; Curtis Gilroy, former Director of Accession Policy within the Office of the Secretary of Defense (Personnel and Readiness); Jeffrey Mayo, former Director of Accession Policy who followed Dr. Gilroy; and, finally, Dennis Drogo, Assistant Director of Military Personnel Policy within the Office of the Under Secretary of Defense (Personnel and Readiness).

We would especially like to thank those at USAFA who provided support for the project, helped with our archival data requests, and offered feedback on earlier drafts of this report, including Brig Gen Dana Born, former dean of the faculty; Col Carolyn Benyshek, director of admissions; Capt Steve Brooks; Phillip Prosseda; Lt Col Patricia Egleston; Col Michael Therianos; Gen Andrew Armacost; Lt Col Adam Marshall; Gail Rosado; Kathleen O'Donnell; Lt Col Robert Ramos; Beth Wilson; and Jau Tsau.

In addition, this project would not have been possible without the support of leadership in the Air Force (including Maj Gen Sharon K. G. Dunbar and Brig Gen Gina M. Grosso, former directors of Force Management Policy, Deputy Chief of Staff for Manpower, Personnel, and Services, Headquarters U.S. Air Force, AF/A1P). We also appreciated the helpful feedback from Lisa Mills, Paul DiTullio, John Park, and Brandon Spillers of AF/A1P, Johnny Weissmuller, John Crown, Laura Barron, Brian Chasse, Gregory Manley, Mark Rose, Kenneth Schwartz of the Air Force Personnel Center, Thomas Carretta of the

Air Force Materiel Command, and Sheila Earle, the former Principal Deputy Assistant Secretary for Manpower and Reserve Affairs.

Judy Mele, Suzy Adler, and Perry Firoz at RAND helped prepare and offered guidance on Air Force career data. Michael Schiefer provided feedback on early analysis work. Capt Jeremy Didier cleaned the data and assisted in analysis. RAND military fellows Col Tim Sipowicz, Col Dave Cox, and Commander Charlene Downey provided key insights along the way. We would also like to thank Jerry Sollinger and Barbara Bicksler for their assistance in formatting and editing this report.

Abbreviations

AIC	Akaike information criterion
ALO	admissions liaison officer
AME	average marginal effect
AP	advanced placement
BIC	Bayesian information criterion
CFA	candidate fitness assessment
DG	Distinguished Graduate
GPA	grade point average
HS	high school
JROTC	Junior Reserve Officer Training Corps
MPA	military performance average
OPA	overall performance average
PAR	prior academic ranking
PEA	physical education average
ROTC	Reserve Officer Training Corps
SD	standard deviation

USAF   United States Air Force

USAFA   United States Air Force Academy

CHAPTER ONE

Introduction

The United States Air Force Academy (USAFA) admissions process is highly competitive.[1] Although the entire admissions process takes many months and includes many factors, final decisions are based on scores calculated as a weighted combination of three elements:

- 60 percent academic composite—includes SAT/ACT score and prior academic ranking (PAR: class rank, grade point average [GPA], transcript, strength of high school, rigor of curriculum)
- 20 percent leadership composite—also called extra-curricular composite; includes activities, leadership, and résumé
- 20 percent selection panel score—selection panel's evaluation of candidate, which includes a review of admissions liaison officer (ALO) evaluations, writing samples, teacher evaluations, recommendations, and the candidate fitness assessment.

The computed total score, called the selection composite score, is used to rank order candidates. Admissions are determined from that score.

This selection formula has been in place for decades, and the result has always been a class of students that is highly respected both within the Air Force and in the educational community. Nevertheless, it is still important to ask, "Can the formula be improved?" We begin

---

[1] Between 2010 and 2014 the number of admissions applications submitted to USAFA ranged from 9,000 to 11,000. Of those that applied in those years, fewer than 20 percent were offered admission.

to address that question in this report through a quantitative examination of how well the elements in the formula above predict outcomes that matter to the U.S. Air Force (USAF).

Desired Outcomes of the Admissions Process

There can be many desired outcomes or goals for a college admissions process. In this study, we focused on three that are particularly relevant for the Air Force as a whole.

Prediction of graduation from USAFA is the first. Although USAFA's admissions process is highly selective, it is only the first of many hurdles that students will encounter, as cadets face not only the traditional academic requirements found at most colleges and universities but also physical and other military-specific challenges. Satisfactory completion of all of USAFA's hurdles and challenges is a prerequisite to completing the degree. Graduation serves as an important prerequisite for entry into the Air Force as an officer. If a USAFA cadet fails to graduate, the cadet is not available to satisfy the commissioning needs of the Air Force. For that reason, identifying who is most likely to complete all four years successfully is one important goal of the admissions process. Recent graduation rates are approximately 75 percent. Improved prediction could increase the number of successful graduates, which could, in turn, result in cost savings for the Air Force.

Prediction of success at USAFA is the second. Those that perform well at USAFA are often viewed as having high potential for success as an Air Force officer. Measures of success at USAFA include military performance average (MPA) and college GPA, which are combined to create USAFA's Order of Merit. The top 10 percent of graduates are awarded Distinguished Graduate (DG) status based on the Order of Merit. Those who receive DG status are highly regarded by the Air Force as exceptional officers and are generally believed to have high potential as future officers. Determining which cadets will be high performers at USAFA is, therefore, another important goal for admissions.

Prediction of who will be a successful officer is the third. All USAFA graduates receive a commission in the Air Force; however, not all are promoted to the higher ranks. Ideally, USAFA's admissions process would identify those applicants who are most likely to be promoted later down the road.

Past Studies Exploring Prediction of USAFA Cadets' Success

This is not the first study to ask how well the admissions factors predict success at USAFA and beyond. For example, Miller (1964) explored the relationship between several predictors (the Air Force Officer Qualifying Test and other academic and nonacademic screening elements) and a variety of USAFA outcomes in the class of 1964. Dempsey and Fast (1976) explored prediction of attrition at USAFA using an interest inventory, prior academic record (including SAT scores, high school GPA and rank, and other academic information), extracurricular activities, and other general background information. Butler and McCauley (1987) reported relationships for both SAT scores and high school rank for the USAFA class of 1983 and the United States Military Academy classes of 1982 and 1983. Valentine (1961) examined prediction of success in pilot training using the Air Force Officer Qualifying Test scores, high school rank, physical aptitude, and other aptitude test scores.

Although all of these studies identified significant relationships between several of the predictors and the outcomes explored and made recommendations for how to adjust the admissions process to improve prediction of success, studies have not been published examining recent cohorts of students or using the key admissions elements that have been in use in recent years. In addition, to the extent that data on those admissions factors are available going back decades, the data permit larger-scale examination of the relationships than could be examined in earlier years and allow for examination of much longer-term outcomes, such as promotion. As a result, there is a gap in the data-driven information that is available to inform policy changes today. Providing this larger-scale examination and exploring prediction of both short-term and long-term outcomes to fill that gap in data-driven solutions were the aims of the work presented here.

Study Approach

In this study, we focused solely on the selection element under USA-FA's discretion: the admissions formula. This is the avenue by which USAFA exercises control over the qualifications of the entering classes, and, therefore, it represents a key area in which policy changes could be made to help improve the quality of those admitted. Other factors, such as the nomination requirement (when congressional members nominate candidates for admissions to the academy), can also have notable impacts on the quality of the entering class. Nevertheless, such factors as congressional nominations are not policy levers under USAFA control.

Although we had in mind a general set of outcomes that we hoped the admissions formula elements would be able to predict (such as performance at USAFA and performance as officers), we did not know at the outset of this study what data would be available for us to use to examine that possibility. We therefore first set out to identify what data were available in existing archival records in the Air Force for use in our predictive validation study and what types of outcomes were generally regarded as important by USAFA and the Air Force as a whole.

Because we aimed to examine the predictive validity of information collected about USAFA applicants (that is, how well that information predicts later outcomes), we looked for data that were obtained about the same people across multiple points in time. We located three archival data sources that could be merged to yield the longitudinal data required for the study: USAFA registrar data collected on people at the time of application to USAFA, academic performance information collected upon graduation from USAFA, and performance data collected after they had been officers in the Air Force for a number of years. After examining the data available to us at these three points in time, we narrowed our study focus to a set of predictors and outcomes: those that were both available in the data sets we identified and considered important by USAFA and/or the Air Force as a whole. The result was a focus on the admissions factors currently in use by USAFA, the more proximal USAFA outcomes (graduation, MPA, GPA, and overall performance average [OPA]), and the more distal officer outcomes (promotions) that we outlined above.

To explore how well the admissions factors predict each of these outcomes (graduation from USAFA, success at USAFA given graduation, and success as an officer), we conducted a variety of statistical regression analyses using the existing archival data provided by the Air Force.

Organization of This Report

Chapter Two provides a brief introduction to the admissions process used by USAFA. Chapter Three provides details on each of the elements involved in USAFA's admissions process. Chapter Four summarizes the data we obtained and the statistical analyses we used to explore the predictive validity of the admissions factors. Chapter Five describes the results of our regression analyses, and Chapter Six presents conclusions and recommendations. We also include supplementary information in two appendixes. Appendix A contains fit indexes and additional statistical output for each of regression models presented in Chapter Four. Appendix B reports the means and standard deviations for our regression model populations.

CHAPTER TWO

Overview of USAFA's Admissions Process and Available Data

Some 10,000 people annually initiate the application process to USAFA. These applications result in about 1,500 candidates being appointed, of whom about 1,200 accept the offer of admission and become cadets. As explained in Chapter One, final decisions about who to accept into USAFA are made on the basis of three scores: the academic composite score, the leadership composite score, and the selection panel score. However, there are many points in the process at which candidates are evaluated. Figure 2.1 shows a flow chart used by USAFA to summarize the various decisions that are made about the applicant. The main components of the application process are listed in Table 2.1. Additional details on each element in the process are provided in the next chapter.

As shown in the figure, the process centers on evaluating the three composite scores. At the beginning of the process, self-report information is collected about the applicant to determine whether an applicant's scores appear competitive. If they do, official scores are requested from the applicant, along with the additional information required for the selection panel. If the self-report information does not appear competitive or if it is incomplete, feedback is provided to the applicant to help him or her determine what improvements to the application materials would be needed.

For those self-reports that are competitive, once official scores are obtained and remaining application requirements have been fulfilled, the information for the selection panel score is gathered and submitted

Figure 2.1
USAFA Selection Process Flow Chart

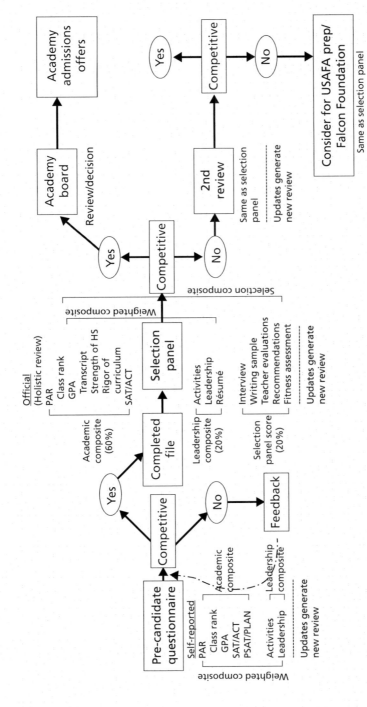

SOURCE: USAFA Selection Panel, Training Briefing for the USAFA class of 2015, undated.
NOTES: PLAN = preliminary version of ACT; PSAT = Preliminary SAT.

RAND RR744-2.1

Table 2.1
Components of the Admissions Process

Item	Description
Pre-candidate questionnaire	Online form used for initial screening
SAT/ACT score[a]	Standardized test scores required for admission
Nomination[a]	From state senator, representative, the Vice President, or the "military-affiliated" category
Candidate fitness assessment[a]	Assesses physical fitness of candidate
Admissions liaison officer interview[a]	Interview with an Air Force officer designated by USAFA
Completed candidate kit	Collection of materials required for admission; includes writing sample, teacher evaluations, and activities record
Medical exam[a]	Candidate must pass a medical examination
Selection panel	A panel of officers at USAFA that reviews the completed candidate kits and rates the candidates
Letter of appointment	Letter from USAFA offering candidate appointment

[a] Becomes part of completed candidate kit.

to the selection panel. Once all three composite scores are available, the final selection composite scores are calculated and submitted to the admissions committee. The end of the process culminates in final offers of admission to USAFA being made to the top candidates, and offers of admission to the Falcon Foundation or the USAFA Preparatory School (Prep School) being made to other candidates of interest.[1]

The overall application process is similar in many ways to that of a civilian university. It involves completing many of the same types of standardized tests, writing samples, and forms as other four-year higher education institutions. Recruiter interview ratings, SAT/ACT scores, writing samples, and teacher letters of recommendation are all required elements. However, the application process also differs in

---

[1]   Because USAFA treats Prep School graduate admissions differently, we excluded anyone who attended the Prep School from all analyses.

some notable ways from that of a typical civilian university. The congressional, military, or presidential nomination requirement; the fitness assessment; and the medical exam are unique to the military academies. The nomination requirement imposes conditions on the selection process that constrain the selection decisions that the academies can ultimately make. As a result, selection of high scorers on the admissions formula is not always possible.[2]

Like most four-year institutions, the timeline for applications can take up to a year from the start of the application process to receipt of the admissions offers. At USAFA, it begins in the second semester of an applicant's junior year and lasts for about 18 months. The timing of each element in the process is shown in Figure 2.2.

USAFA Archival Data

As indicated in Figure 2.1, many pieces of information about USAFA's applicants are collected during the application process and ultimately combined to yield a final USAFA admission decision. However, we discovered during this study that individual scores and other information on many key elements are not necessarily retained in the Air Force's existing archival data sources, and many of those that are retained are recorded inconsistently or use codebooks that have not been maintained over the years. Additionally, some elements (such as written personal statements or letters of recommendation) existed in paper form only and were never entered into an electronic database. As a result, through our efforts to uncover and interpret the existing data archived at USAFA, we have identified a number of ways that recordkeeping and data maintenance could be improved to assist in validation studies like ours in the future. These, along with our other recommendations, are discussed in Chapter Six.

---

[2]   About half of the USAFA class is selected from the congressional nomination process, in which a candidate may be competing against only a handful of other candidates. In addition, when principal nominees who meet minimum requirements are named, they must be offered admission even if they have lower admissions formula scores than other candidates. As a result, it is not possible for USAFA to establish a clear-cut line on the admissions formula.

Figure 2.2
Admissions Timeline

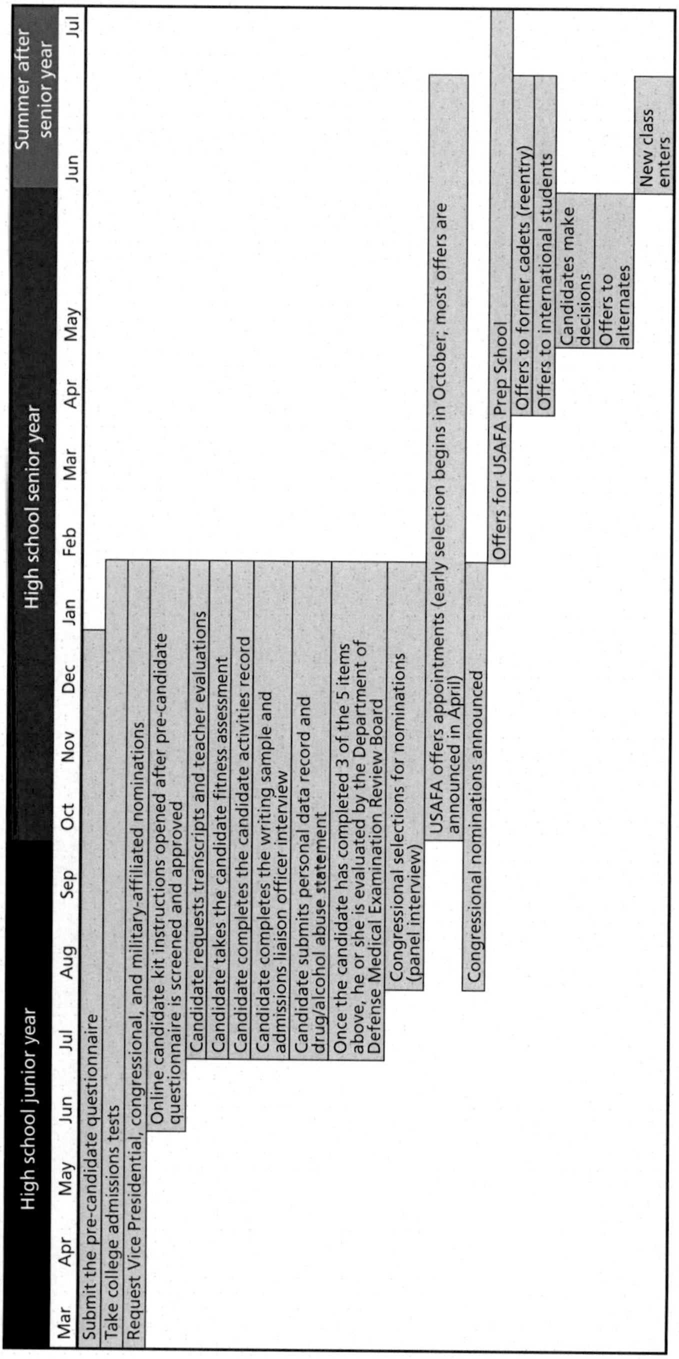

	High school junior year										High school senior year						Summer after senior year	
	Mar	Apr	May	Jun	Jul	Aug	Sep	Oct	Nov	Dec	Jan	Feb	Mar	Apr	May	Jun	Jul

Submit the pre-candidate questionnaire

Take college admissions tests

Request Vice Presidential, congressional, and military-affiliated nominations

Online candidate kit instructions opened after pre-candidate questionnaire is screened and approved

Candidate requests transcripts and teacher evaluations

Candidate takes the candidate fitness assessment

Candidate completes the candidate activities record

Candidate completes the writing sample and admissions liaison officer interview

Candidate submits personal data record and drug/alcohol abuse statement

Once the candidate has completed 3 of the 5 items above, he or she is evaluated by the Department of Defense Medical Examination Review Board

Congressional selections for nominations (panel interview)

Congressional nominations announced

USAFA offers appointments (early selection begins in October; most offers are announced in April)

Offers for USAFA Prep School

Offers to former cadets (reentry)

Offers to international students

Candidates make decisions

Offers to alternates

New class enters

SOURCES: United States Air Force, 2010; United States Air Force Academy, 2010b; United States Air Force Academy, 2012.

RAND RR744-2.2

Regardless of the existing data shortfalls, scores on the three elements that were used to compute USAFA's selection composite scores (the central elements in their accessions process) have been maintained on everyone admitted to USAFA for the last three decades. This fit with the goal of our study, which was to use a predictive validation design to examine the validity of the information that was known about applicants at the time at which they were applying to USAFA. In other words, we wanted to assess the extent to which the current method of using the information collected from USAFA applicants to determine admission is justified by evidence—that is, does this method result in a pool of applicants who are successful at USAFA as well as in their careers as U.S. Air Force officers? These three composite scores were, therefore, the factors on which we focused in this study.

Components of the Admissions Process

In this chapter, we provide a detailed description of each of the elements required in the admissions process.

Pre-Candidate Questionnaire

This questionnaire is the initial step in gaining admission to USAFA. The questionnaire is filled out online and is designed to gauge an individual's potential for admission. To be eligible, an individual must meet the following requirements:[1]

- be a United States citizen
- be unmarried without dependents
- be at least 17 and not have passed his or her 23rd birthday on July 1 of the year he or she enters USAFA.

The bar against dependents includes not only a spouse by marriage and a biological child but also stepchildren or adopted children, regardless of whether the individual is supporting these children.[2] An individual need not be a citizen when first applying, but citizenship must be finalized before entry.

---

[1] USAFA does admit international students; however, admissions for those students are determined using a different process and different set of eligibility criteria.

[2] Candidates may be eligible if they have children, but they must give up all parental rights and must have no obligation to support them financially.

The individual must also meet a personal standards require-ment. The applicant must be able to explain any of the following cir-cumstances: periods as a conscientious objector; if the appointment is inconsistent with national security interests; conviction by court-martial if other than a "minor offense" or conviction of a felony in civilian court; elimination from a military officer training or a federal service academy for military inaptitude, indifference, or undesirable traits of character; habitual alcohol misuse or drug abuse that exceeds Air Force standards; or behavior, activity, or association showing that the applicant's conduct is incompatible with exemplary standards of personal conduct, moral character, and integrity.

The pre-candidate questionnaire also solicits information about academic performance, as measured by GPA, class standing, and scores on standardized tests—i.e., the SAT and ACT. Preliminary SAT (PSAT) scores or PLAN (a test taken in 10th grade to prepare for the ACT) scores may be submitted with the pre-candidate ques-tionnaire, but the SAT or ACT (or both) must be submitted as part of the completed candidate kit. Those completing the pre-candidate questionnaire and meeting the admission standards become "tentative candidates." Tentative candidates are mailed information on how to access additional forms online—the candidate kit—which is needed to continue the application process.

SAT and ACT

The SAT and the ACT are standardized tests used in the admissions process of most colleges and universities.[3] These may be taken mul-tiple times. Scores become part of the complete admissions kit, and USAFA will consider the highest scores on each component of the test. Table 3.1 shows the average scores on the SAT and ACT for the USAFA classes of 2012–2014.

---

3   ACT and SAT are the official names of the tests (i.e., they are not acronyms).

Table 3.1
Average SAT, ACT, and High School GPA Scores for USAFA Attendees (Classes 2012–2014)

	Graduating Class Year		
	2012	2013	2014
Mean SAT Verbal	642	639	640
Mean SAT Math	663	664	666
Mean ACT English	29.0	29.6	29.7
Mean ACT Math	29.7	30.3	30.3
Mean ACT Reading	30.0	30.1	30.3
Mean ACT Science Reasoning	29.1	29.4	29.7
HS GPA	3.86	3.86	3.87

SOURCES: United States Air Force Academy, 2008, 2009, 2010a.

NOTES: Class refers to the expected graduating year. Data exclude USAFA Prep School graduates and international cadets. Maximum SAT score is 800 per subject. Maximum ACT score is 36. Although high school (HS) GPA in the earlier years of our data was uninterpretable (it ranged from 0.00 to 10.00), for 2012 through 2014 it was within an interpretable range (it ranged from 0.00 to 5.00).

Nomination

Admittance to USAFA requires a nomination from one of three categories. Each United States senator and representative has an allotted number of nominations he or she can use to nominate individuals to USAFA. Those nominations are awarded to individuals applying to USAFA from the state or district of the senator or representative. A second category is that of the Vice President, who can nominate candidates from the nation at large. A third category is military-affiliated nominations, which includes many subcategories. These include presidential nominations, which the President of the United States can award to children of career military personnel. Another subcategory is children of deceased or disabled veterans (disability rating must be 100 percent). An additional subcategory is children of Medal of Honor recipients. Yet another subcategory for military-affiliated nominations is honor military schools and Air Force Reserve Officer Training Corps (ROTC). Honor military schools are so designated by the departments of the Army, Marine Corps, and Navy to nominate candidates to USAFA from among their honor students. Members of high school and college Air Force ROTC honor units may apply for nomination. The final subcategory includes the regular airman nomination categories (for which regular airmen are eligible) and reserve airman nomination categories (for which reserve and guard members are eligible).

Applicants are encouraged to apply for a nomination in all relevant categories. Members of Congress (House of Representatives and Senate) make nominations from August 1 through January 31, with some closing out nominations as early as October. January 31 is also the deadline for nomination requests to be sent to the Vice President and for military-affiliated nomination requests. The applicant becomes a "candidate" when he or she receives this service academy nomination.

Candidate Fitness Assessment

The candidate fitness assessment (CFA) assesses the physical capabilities of a candidate. It is a proctored physical fitness exam that has six components: a basketball throw, pull-ups, a shuttle run, modified sit-ups, push-ups, and a one-mile run. The test is administered by a member of the physical education department of the candidate's high school, a liaison officer to USAFA, or an Air Force Junior Reserve Officer Training Corps (JROTC) instructor. Each test element is designed to test different physical or motor skills, and the entire test must be completed at a single session within specified time limits. Scores and their certifications become part of the completed candidate kit. Table 3.2 lists the average scores by event and gender for the various components assessed in the CFA.

Table 3.2
Mean Entering Candidate Performance Scores by Event and Gender

	Male	Female
Basketball throw	69 ft.	41 ft.
Pull-ups	11	3
Shuttle run	8.8s	9.7s
Modified sit-ups	79	78
Push-ups	60	41
1-mile run	6m 41s	7m 44s

SOURCE: United States Air Force Academy, 2010b.

Admissions Liaison Officer Interview

ALOs are a cadre of Air Force Reserve, Air National Guard, active duty, and retired officers and civilians who participate in the admissions process by counseling and interviewing candidates. They are situated around the country, and the candidate is charged to make contact with one in his or her region. USAFA encourages multiple contacts with the ALO, but only one is required. That requirement is a formal interview that the liaison officer conducts and reports on to USAFA.

Completed Candidate Kit

The applicant is encouraged to complete his or her "admissions file" as early as possible. This allows the candidate to be considered for appointment as early as October. The candidate officially has until January 31 to complete his or her file. The forms and evaluations required for admission to USAFA are listed in Table 3.3 and are described in detail in the paragraphs that follow.

Table 3.3
Components of Candidate Kit

Item
School official's evaluation of candidate
Candidate personal data record
Candidate activities record
Request for secondary transcript
Preparatory school and college transcripts
Writing sample
Drug and alcohol abuse certificate

The candidate is required to submit a writing sample, which is guided by prompts established by USAFA. The following are example prompts from previous admissions years (the ones used today are different):

Write 250–300 words on one of the following prompts:

- When did you first become interested in the Air Force Academy and serving in the Air Force? What started your interest? What Air Force career field do you hope to enter? What do you expect to gain from the Air Force Academy experience and how will it help you in your Air Force career?

--Or--

- Which aspect of the Air Force Academy experience (academic, military training, athletic, social/spiritual) do you anticipate will be most challenging for you? Discuss why and how you expect to succeed in that area.

And write 400–500 words on the following prompt:

- Describe a setback or ethical dilemma that you have faced. How did you resolve it? How did the outcome affect you? If something similar happens in the future, how would you react?

The applicant must have an English teacher, a math teacher, and another teacher (science is suggested, but the applicant decides) submit a U.S. Air Force Academy School Officials Evaluation of Candidate form (United States Air Force Academy, 2006a).[4] The teachers must have taught the applicant in the junior or senior year. This form asks the evaluator to rate the candidate across 12 categories using the following rating scale: top 1 percent, top 10 percent, above average, average, below average, or not observed. Examples of the categories are "works toward group goals when in a subordinate position," "demonstrates personal integrity," and "accepts personal responsibility for own actions." The teacher is also asked to comment on the applicant's academic performance (including how he or she compares with the teacher's other students), about any special circumstances in the applicant's background, any accomplishments or circumstances that make the applicant exceptional, and any traits the applicant is known for. In addition to this form, the applicant is encouraged (but not required) to submit up to three letters of recommendation from people who can speak to the student's "character, integrity, leadership abilities and experience" (United States Air Force Academy, 2010b).

The applicant also must have a school official complete the Air Force Academy Request for Secondary School Transcript.[5] In addition to submitting the student's transcript, the school official is also asked to provide the applicant's cumulative GPA,[6] the GPA scale at the school, the student's class rank (or percentile if rank is not available), the number of students in the class, the number of semesters included in the class rank or GPA calculation, the percentage of the graduating class expected to enter two-year and four-year colleges, if the student took honors courses or advanced placement (AP) courses, if honors

---

[4] If the student is homeschooled, he or she can have an individual from his or her community who knows him or her well complete the form. If the applicant is in college, he or she can have college professors complete the form.

[5] If the applicant is a current college student or preparatory student, he or she must also submit college/preparatory school transcripts. Homeschooled students must also submit a transcript.

[6] The average GPAs for USAFA classes of 2012–2014 were 3.86, 3.86, and 3.87, respectively (United States Air Force Academy, 2008, 2009, 2010a).

courses or AP courses factor into GPA or class rank calculations, and to rate the difficulty of the student's curriculum based on available courses. The school official is also requested to provide the ranking period and to provide the school's grading scale (i.e., what is signified by an A, B, C, or D) (United States Air Force Academy, 2007).

The student must also have a school official fill out the USAF Academy School Profile. This form asks questions regarding the student population (e.g., "percent of students who come from socio-economically disadvantaged homes"), academics (e.g., "number of AP courses offered at your school"), the student's senior year schedule, and the school's setting (i.e., urban, rural, suburban) (United States Air Force Academy, 2007).

The student must fill out the Air Force Academy Candidate Activities Record. This form has two sections: athletic activities and nonathletic activities. In the athletic activities section, the school official is asked to indicate in which grade (10–12) the student participated in the activity; earned a varsity letter; was team captain or co-captain; or was all-state, all-district, all-city, or all-county. The nonathletic section asks questions about school/nonschool officer positions, school/nonschool publications, awards and honors (e.g., national honor society, academic bowl team, etc.), work (summer job, hours worked per week, etc.), music participation, other high school/community activities (JROTC, debate team, community service, etc.), youth organizations (Boy or Girl Scouts, Camp Fire, etc.), civil air patrol participation, and working toward a pilot's license. In addition to this form, the applicant must fill out a résumé in which he or she can list anything not included in the form or expand on what is included (United States Air Force Academy, 2003b).

The applicant is asked to fill out the Air Force Academy Candidate Personal Data Record. This form asks questions about the candidate, including citizenship, gender, race, date of birth, parental information (includes military status), disciplinary actions at school, criminal activity, family income, and service record (United States Air Force Academy, 2003a).

The applicant must fill out the USAF Drug and Alcohol Abuse Certificate. This form has three sections. The first provides the applicant with definitions of terms used in the form. The second is a "certification at time of application" which asks the applicant about previous drug use or involvement with drugs. The third section is "statements of understanding," asking the student to verify that he or she understands the drug and alcohol policies of USAFA (United States Air Force, 1999).

The applicant must also submit the USAF Academy Candidate Fitness Assessment Exam Score Sheet. The form has a section in which the examiner can explain unusual circumstances and in which the applicant can make remarks (United States Air Force Academy, 2006b).

Medical Examination

The applicant must also schedule a medical exam with the Department of Defense Medical Examination Review Board. This process can take over three weeks if there are no complications, but it can take up to four months if the applicant has to retest or must have waivers approved. It is recommended that the student takes this exam as soon as possible, but results can be submitted from July through March.

Selection Panel

Once a candidate's application package is completed and received, it is sent to the Selection Panel. This panel meets weekly from October through March. It is composed of USAFA faculty and staff and is chaired by an Air Force colonel. One member of the panel reviews each application and awards it a panel score. The panel chair then reviews these scores. All scores are combined into a selection composite, which is then passed on to the USAFA board.

The USAFA board, composed of the senior USAFA officers, meets every week to approve appointments. The board also has the authority to make decisions on exceptions to the general selection rule, based on USAFA's current needs. Applicants granted appointments by the board are sent offers of appointment. Around 1,500 offers of admission are made each year, with some 1,300 in the entering class. Table 3.1 showed the class profiles for the classes of 2012–2014. Table 3.2 listed the mean performance on the CFA for men and women who enter USAFA.

Statistical Approach and Data Sources

Data Sources and Variables

Our data included the nearly 35,000 cadets who attended USAFA from 1980 through 2011. The data were pulled from three Air Force data sources.

USAFA Registrar Admissions Records

USAFA retains data on all applicants who are offered admissions to USAFA. These registrar records contained the selection factors we used in predicting later USAFA and officer success. All electronic records on applicants and selectees retained from 1980 through 2011 were provided for use in this study.

Although these records contained several potentially interesting elements that could be useful additions to the existing selection composites, we excluded many of them from the analyses because of quality concerns. Those for which the data were missing over several years, those with low base rates (such as being a team captain), and those that had a large number of uninterpretable values (e.g., high school GPAs spread across a range from 0.00 to 10.00) were excluded from our final set of variables. This resulted in our focusing on the following variables in our analyses:

- SAT/ACT composite scores
- HS rank divided by class size (hereafter referred to simply as HS rank)
- selection composite score

- leadership composite score
- academic composite score
- selection panel score.

As a reminder, all of the above variables contribute to the existing USAFA admissions formula described in Chapter One. USAFA's admissions decisions are made based on the selection composite score, which is a weighted combination of the leadership composite, academic composite, and selection panel scores. SAT scores[1] are combined with other academic factors (like HS GPA and HS rank) to produce the academic composite.[2] Although both HS rank and GPA contribute to the academic composite, we included only HS rank in our analyses because, as noted above, the range of GPAs (0.00 to 10.00) in our data was not interpretable. However, HS rank can also serve as a proxy for GPA, and we therefore treat it as such in our discussion of the analyses. We explored the six variables above, which we refer to collectively as the *admissions criteria*, as predictors of the USAFA and officer outcomes defined below.

USAFA Cadet Records

USAFA retains data on several aspects of cadet performance at USAFA. Of those, four stood out as being highly valued by USAFA and the Air Force. We selected those as the key USAFA outcomes to be predicted in our regression analyses:

- graduation
- cumulative college GPA
- OPA
- MPA.

---

[1]   For our analyses, we recentered both SAT and ACT scores where appropriate. Then, for those cadets who took the ACT and not the SAT, the ACT scores were converted to equivalent SAT scores using concordance tables. For more on recentering and concordance tables see College Board, 2015a and 2015b.

[2]   Note that some high schools do not calculate an HS rank. Nevertheless, within the data provided to us by USAFA, the HS rank and school size information was fairly complete.

We refer to these collectively as *USAFA outcomes*.

Cadet records from 1980 through 2011 on these four USAFA outcomes were merged with the admissions criteria defined above. Cadets admitted after 2007 would not have been eligible to graduate by 2011. We excluded one additional year (to account for the possibility of unanticipated graduation delays) and limited our analyses of USAFA outcomes to cohorts from 2006 and earlier.

Air Force Personnel Records

Personnel data records from 1981 through 2011 obtained from the Air Force Personnel Center served as our third source of data. The data were merged with USAFA files described above. We used the following variables in our analyses:

- date of commission
- date of promotion to O-4, O-5, and O-6
- career field grouping.

Date of commission was used to establish a person's entry cohort year. Cohorts that had not been in the service for long enough to be considered for a given promotion were excluded from that set of promotions analysis. Based on the overall rates of promotion in our data, we identified the following cohort years as cutoffs for our analyses: up to 1990 for O-6, 1996 for O-5, and 1990 for O-4.[3]

We opted to use promotions in these analyses as a proxy for job performance[4] because a suitable measure of job performance does not currently exist in the personnel data.[5] Date of promotion was used to

---

[3]   We used 1990 as the cutoff for O-4 promotions because there was too little variation in promotion rates for those in the 1990 cohort and later who met an O-4 promotion board.

[4]   The decision to use promotions as a proxy for performance assumes that those who are promoted are better performers than those who are not promoted. Although the Air Force's promotions process is believed to distinguish between higher and lower performers and, therefore, would serve as a suitable proxy measure of performance, this is an untested assumption.

[5]   Officer performance ratings are collected and retained in the personnel system; however, the scores have almost no variance and are therefore of little value in regression analyses.

determine whether personnel received a promotion to O-4, O-5, or O-6, when eligible. All individuals who left the service before they were eligible for promotion, or who did not see a promotion board, were excluded from the promotions analyses. We refer to these proxy measures of performance collectively as our measures of *officer outcomes* in the analyses described below.

We used career field grouping to limit our promotions analyses to line officers only. Because promotions can occur at different rates in the rated community relative to the nonrated community, we present promotions analyses separately for each.[6]

Statistical Regression Analyses

Our analyses used statistical regression techniques to examine the validity of USAFA's admissions variables for predicting the USAFA and officer outcomes.[7] The analyses follow a predictive validation design, in which data collected on people applying to an organization are used to predict important organizational outcomes after they have joined the organization. This approach has been used widely for validating admissions criteria in other higher education contexts (for a few examples, see Lievens, Buyse, and Sackett, 2005; Kulatunga Moruzi and Norman, 2002; and Geiser and Santelices, 2007). It is also consistent with recommended best practice for the validation of selection practices in both educational and workplace settings, as outlined by

---

[6] Although we explored using additional career field groupings in our regressions (i.e., two-digit Air Force Specialty Code), we discovered that the findings did not differ when those controls were used. In nearly all cases, it did not produce significant improvements in the fit of our models. In the few cases in which it did, the change in the weights for the other predictors was negligible.

[7] Statistical regression is the standard method for examining predictive validity in educational and employment settings. For more on recommended best practices for validating selection systems, see *Principles for the Validation and Use of Personnel Selection Procedures* (Society for Industrial and Organizational Psychology, 2003) and *Standards for Educational and Psychological Testing* (Joint Committee on Standards for Educational and Psychological Testing, 1999).

the Society for Industrial and Organizational Psychology (2003) and the American Educational Research Association et al. (2014).

In this study, we use USAFA admissions data to predict a person's success at USAFA four years later (i.e., graduation and performance at USAFA) and success as an officer years after commissioning (i.e., promotions). In the three sections that follow, we define the statistical models used to explore this predictive validation design, discuss how the findings of the models can be used to inform USAFA admissions policies, and describe some of the methodological limitations of our analyses.

Defining the Regression Models

We used logistic regression for predicting the dichotomous outcomes (graduation and promotions) and linear regression for predicting GPA, MPA, and OPA. For all outcomes, we compared a series of regression models. The first three models examined the predictive validity of the information available on candidates at the time of their application to USAFA.

- *Model 1 included four predictors: HS rank, SAT,*[8] *leadership composite, and selection panel score.* This model allowed us to examine the predictive value of SAT and HS rank using data-driven regression weights and to compare the results to those of Model 2.
- *Model 2 included these three predictors: academic composite, leadership composite, and selection panel score.* This model allowed us to estimate the best-fitting weights for the three composite scores used in USAFA admissions. It also allowed us to determine whether an optimal weighting of SAT and HS rank (found in Model 1) would be an improvement over USAFA's existing academic composite (found in Model 2).
- *Model 3 included one predictor: the selection composite score.* The selection composite is the final score that was used by USAFA to make admissions decisions. By comparing statistical fit indexes

---

[8]   Because academic composite is calculated using SAT and GPA, it is excluded from this model.

for Model 3 to Models 1 and 2, we can explore whether the first two models suggest that improvements could be made to USA-FA's admissions formula.

We also included two additional models to examine how well USAFA outcomes predict later officer success.

- *Model 4 included two predictors: MPA and GPA.* These are the two main elements of USAFA's OPA. OPA represents USAFA's order of merit score, which is used to award the top 10 percent of USAFA graduates the title of Distinguished Graduate.
- *Model 5 included one predictor: OPA.*[9] Comparison of Model 5 to Model 4 allowed us to examine the predictive validity of USAFA's current order of merit and identify whether adjustments to the current weighting of MPA and GPA could yield a more predictive order of merit score.

In the analyses presented in the main body of the report, we standardized the predictors and outcomes before computing the regression results.[10] When standardized, each regression coefficient represents the amount of change in the outcome associated with a one-standard-deviation increase in the predictor. For the linear regression analyses, we report R-squared values as a measure of model fit and only describe R-squared values as significantly higher than other models when the difference still remained after accounting for shrinkage due to overfitting.[11] For the logistic regression analyses, we examined model fit using

---

[9]   OPA is a linear combination of MPA and GPA; therefore, it cannot be included in the same model as these two predictors.

[10]   Standardizing the variables allows us to compare regression weights across predictors using a common scale of measurement. Unstandardized regression results reported as average marginal effects for the logistic regressions and unstandardized beta coefficients for the linear regressions are provided in Appendix A.

[11]   To examine whether the R-squared values were higher simply due to overfitting, we applied a Copas test and examined shrinkage in R-squared by splitting the sample into a training sample (used to create a set of training beta weights) and a holdout sample (used to evaluate the fit of the training beta weights). We repeated the process 100 times and computed the average of the R-squared values obtained on each of the holdout samples. If a mod-

the log-likelihood, the Akaike information criterion (AIC), and the Bayesian information criterion (BIC).[12] Log-likelihood, AIC, and BIC statistics are reported in the appendixes.

In several places in the main body of the report, we note the model with the lowest AIC and BIC statistics and describe it as the best-fitting model out of the models we considered. When conclusions based on AIC and BIC differed, we do not describe that model as having a better fit relative to the other models.

Policy Implications of the Regression Models

These five statistical models can be used to inform USAFA admissions policy in three ways.

- **Examination of a single model can help identify the most appropriate weight for each selection variable when the goal is prediction of a certain outcome.** For example, if prediction of GPA is the goal, the best-fitting weights for three primary selection factors (academic composite, leadership composite, and selection panel score) could be found in Model 2 for predicting GPA.
- **Comparing across models that use different admissions factors to predict the same outcome can show whether changing the contents of the USAFA formula could lead to improvements.** For example, by comparing the statistics from Model 3 to Models 1 and 2, we can determine which admissions elements do the best job of predicting a given outcome. Similarly, comparing statistics from Model 4 to Model 5 tells us whether there could be improvements made to the order of merit formula.
- **Comparing the results for prediction of different outcomes can help identify which outcomes are least well predicted by the existing admissions factors. This can help guide the devel-**

---

el's average holdout R-squared value is still higher than that of the other models, it suggests that the improvement is not solely due to overfitting. In this report, we describe models as having significant improvement over other models only when the Copas test and the average R-squared values of the holdout samples supported that conclusion. For more discussion on overfitting, see Copas (1983).

[12] For an example discussion on the use of AIC and BIC for model fit, see Kuha (2004).

opment of entirely new selection factors. Comparing which of the important outcomes (graduation, GPA, promotion, etc.) are best predicted by any combination of the existing selection factors and which outcomes are not as well predicted can suggest areas where the development of new selection factors should be explored. These and other conceptual interpretations of the findings are discussed more in the following chapters.

A Note on the Impact of Policy and Data Constraints and on the Analyses

There are important nuances in the USAFA admissions process that serve to limit the policy implications of the statistical analyses presented here. One is that there are several constraints and selection practices that prevent the process from being a purely meritocratic system. The guaranteed admittance for a congressional nominee who meets only the minimum requirements is one example. The use of Vice Presidential nominations to bring in students to fill important niche positions, such as student athletes, is another. Both of these avenues for admitting students can occur without consideration of a candidate's ranking on the USAFA admissions formula.

A second nuance is USAFA's use of graduation order of merit to determine entry into certain Air Force career pathways that offer higher probabilities for advancement (e.g., pilot training). This could lead to artificially inflated statistical relationships between the predictors and outcomes, a phenomenon referred to in the academic research literature as *criterion contamination* (see, for example, Brogden and Taylor, 1950). This criterion contamination could lead to limitations in interpretation of the analysis results for the Air Force outcome variables.

A third nuance relates to the quality and content of the existing archival data sources. That quality and content significantly limited what could be explored in this study in several ways. Among the absent elements was information on those who are rejected from USAFA. It is well established that the magnitude of statistical relationships can be significantly underestimated when the range of scores is narrower in the group that is selected than it is in the applicant population. Although there are corrections that can be applied to correct for those differences (see, for example, Sackett and Yang, 2000), the standard deviations of the selected group and the applicant pool must be known. Unfortunately, in this case, we have usable data only on people who were admitted. Although this prevents us from applying corrections for range restriction, we suspect that the amount of direct range restriction occurring in our population is less than might be expected in some selection contexts. The congressional nomination processes, for example, are not decided on the basis of the admissions formula and therefore help to increase the variance in the admissions scores of people who are selected. Nevertheless, having access to data on rejected applicants could help address this issue in future research.

Other archival information was incomprehensible (such as HS GPA), which prevented us from using certain data elements in our study. And there were many subscore elements that were not recorded or retained in USAFA archival data sets (such as prior academic record elements and SAT subscores), which could therefore not be explored as potential predictors of USAFA or officer outcomes. This need for increased data collection and better recordkeeping is discussed further in our recommendations.

CHAPTER FIVE

Regression Analysis Results

This chapter summarizes the results of our regression analyses for three sets of outcomes. The first set of outcomes focuses on graduation. Because considerable resources are spent on USAFA cadets during their four years of education, selecting or admitting those who will graduate is an important goal for the admissions process. As we discovered in our data, USAFA graduates only about 75 percent of its entering class. There is no magic number for an ideal graduation rate; however, we presume that the people who are not graduating are failing to do so because they do not meet certain criteria or minimum levels of performance expected by the university. As such, the university could improve upon that rate if more of its students succeeded at meeting those criteria and performance standards. Such improvements in success rates would then translate to a greater return on the overall USAFA educational investment. Thus, aiming for an even higher graduation rate is a worthwhile policy goal.

Of those who did not graduate, 18 percent failed to do so for academic reasons (such as not passing classes or meeting minimum GPA requirements), whereas 41 percent simply decided that an Air Force career was not for them.[1] With graduation as a necessary condition for becoming a commissioned officer, prediction of both success in the curriculum and a willingness to continue in an Air Force career should be important aims for the admissions process. Policy decisions regard-

---

[1] The remaining 41 percent left for a wide variety of other voluntary and involuntary reasons, including adjustment problems, honor code violations, medical or physical fitness issues, and conduct violations.

ing the factors included in the selection process should take these outcomes into account. Moreover, given that rates of attrition are twice as high for a leaving for a career change as they are for failure due to academic reasons, failure to graduate because someone desires a career change could be one area in which policy changes to the selection formula could have the greatest positive impact. Adjusting the weights in the admissions formula to better predict these outcomes would therefore be an important policy change for USAFA to consider.

In the first section below, we explore how well our regression models predict those two graduation outcomes: graduation versus failure for academic reasons and graduation versus desiring a career change. For both graduation outcomes, we included anyone who was admitted to USAFA and listed as a member of the 1980 through 2011 graduation cohorts.[2]

We next explore the prediction of three other important USAFA outcomes: cumulative GPA, cumulative MPA, and cumulative OPA. Cumulative GPA is the average of the grades received in all college courses completed during a cadet's four years, weighted by credit hour, at USAFA. MPA ratings are collected from a wide variety of sources over a cadet's time at USAFA, including instructors, coaches, and officers in charge. They also incorporate scores from a number of other variables, some of which are the result of demerit counts; peer, upperclass, and Air Officer Commanding evaluations of military merit; and grades in military courses. The content of the ratings includes assessments of a cadet's ability to communicate, encourage teamwork, motivate subordinates, accomplish assigned missions, inspire others, and resolve conflict (Didier, 2012), as well as his or her military bearing, job performance, professional knowledge, personal appearance, initiative, attitude, and leadership ability (USAFA, Association of Graduates, 2012). OPA is used by USAFA as an assessment of overall cadet success. Prior to the class of 2009, it was calculated as 70 percent GPA and 30 percent MPA. For the class of 2009 onward, it has been calculated as 60 percent GPA, 30 percent MPA, and 10 percent cumulative

---

2   People entering USAFA after 2006 would not have been eligible to graduate by 2011 and are therefore excluded.

physical education average (PEA). OPA serves as USAFA's Order of Merit, which is used to determine Distinguished Graduate status.

In the last section below, we explore prediction of promotions to major (O-4), lt. colonel (O-5), and colonel (O-6) for rated and non-rated officers. We first examine how well the admissions factors predicted these promotion outcomes, and we then explore how well the USAFA outcome measures (MPA, GPA, and OPA) predict the same set of promotion outcomes.

Predicting USAFA Graduation

As a reminder, for all of the analyses presented below, the best-fitting weights for each predictor in the model are reported in standardized units. Weights significantly higher than zero (alpha level 0.05) are noted with an asterisk.

Graduation Versus Failure for Academic Reasons

Table 5.1 displays the results for all three models predicting graduation versus failure to graduate for academic reasons.

Overall, the admissions factors in Models 1 through 3 are useful predictors of who graduates versus who fails to graduate for academic reasons. The standardized beta weights are significant for all of the predictors included in Models 1 through 3.

Also, nearly all of the predictors included appear to be useful for predicting graduation. Model 1 shows that SAT is a significant predictor, with higher scores associated with a higher likelihood of graduating. HS rank is also a significant predictor in the direction we would expect (as HS rank goes down, likelihood of graduating goes up), and leadership composite is a significant predictor in the direction we would expect as well. In Model 2, academic composite, which includes HS GPA and SAT scores, is also shown to be a strong significant predictor. Lastly, in Model 3, selection composite is a significant predictor.

Selection panel score, however, is the one exception. In both Models 1 and 2, it is significant, but in the wrong direction: Higher

Table 5.1
Predicting Graduating Versus Not Graduating for Academic Reasons

	Model 1	Model 2	Model 3
HS rank/size	−0.11*		
SAT composite	0.21*		
Academic composite		0.40*	
Leadership composite	0.10*	0.08*	
Selection panel score	−0.14*	−0.09*	
Selection composite			0.22*

NOTES: N = 22,375. All regression models are significant at $p <$ 0.001. Coefficients marked with an asterisk (*) are significant at $p < 0.05$. Results are reported in standardized units. For each predictor, the weight displayed indicates the average amount of change in the outcome that is associated with a one-standard-deviation change in the predictor. Standard errors for regression coefficients ranged from < 0.01 to 0.01.

scores are associated with a lower likelihood of graduating.[3] In light of this, we examined whether adding an interaction term (where each factor in the model is multiplied by the selection panel score) would impact the results and found that doing so did not change the findings. The main effect for selection panel score was still negative and significant, and the interaction terms were not significant.

A comparison of all three models suggests that the current weights used by USAFA in computing the selection composite are effective, but it also shows they could be improved for predicting graduation versus not graduating for academic reasons. Fit indexes show that all three models are significant predictors of who fails to graduate for academic reasons (chi-squared p-value < 0.05). However, the AIC and BIC fit indexes (reported in Appendix B) show that Models 1 and 2 are significantly better than Model 3, and that Model 2 is the best of the

---

[3]   This finding is replicated in nearly all analyses in this chapter. It is discussed in greater detail in the conclusions.

three. This indicates that a change to the selection composite formula to use the weights similar to those suggested in Model 2 could result in improved prediction of graduation versus failure for academic reasons.

If USAFA were to adopt the formula suggested by Model 2, the weight for academic composite would be quite large relative to the weight for the leadership composite. The standardized coefficient shows the increase in the likelihood of graduating that corresponds to a one-standard-deviation increase in the predictor. By standardizing the predictors, we can compare the weights across predictors on a common scale. For example, in Model 1, SAT has about twice the weight of HS rank or leadership composite (0.21 versus 0.11 or 0.10), and according to Model 2, the suggested weight for the academic composite would be about five times the weight of the leadership composite.[4]

Graduation Versus Leaving for a Career Change

Results for graduating versus not graduating because of a desire for a career change are shown in Table 5.2.

Several of the findings for predicting this graduation outcome are similar to those for the previous graduation outcome. For example, selection panel score predicts graduation versus choosing a career change, but not in the expected direction; SAT, academic composite, and leadership composite are significant predictors in the expected direction; all three models have significant chi-squared values ($p < 0.05$); and Model 2 is again better than all other models (see fit indexes in Appendix B for more information).

However, there are also some notable differences between these results and those presented above. First, the weight for HS rank is not statistically significant. Second, the standardized weights for the

---

[4]   Although standardization allows for a simplified comparison of relative weights across predictors, the application of those relative weights to unstandardized data is more complex. Because the magnitude comparisons only apply after standardizing the variables to have the same mean and standard deviation, using the standardized weights to make changes to the admissions formula would require that the formula also incorporate the same mean and standard deviation transformations used in these regressions. The means and standard deviations reported in Appendix B can be used to approximate those transformations. Alternatively, the unstandardized regression weights reported as average marginal effects in Appendix A could also be used without requiring any transformation.

Table 5.2
Predicting Graduating Versus Not Graduating for Career Change Reasons

	Model 1	Model 2	Model 3
HS rank/size	−0.02		
SAT composite	0.04*		
Academic composite		0.10*	
Leadership composite	0.08*	0.08*	
Selection panel score	−0.16*	−0.15*	
Selection composite			0.04

NOTES: $N = 23{,}358$. All regression models are significant at $p < 0.001$. Coefficients marked with an asterisk (*) are significant at $p < 0.05$. Results are reported in standardized units. For each predictor, the weight displayed indicates the average amount of change in the outcome that is associated with a one-standard-deviation change in the predictor. Standard errors for regression coefficients ranged from < 0.01 to 0.01.

remainder of the predictors are all much smaller in magnitude, and according to the fit indexes located in Appendix B, none of the three models do as good of a job at predicting this graduation outcome as they did at predicting graduation versus not graduating for academic reasons. Put simply, these predictors are not as useful for predicting nongraduation for career change reasons as they are for academic reasons.[5]

---

[5]   Although the regression coefficients in the analysis predicting graduation versus academic failure are noticeably higher than those for predicting graduation versus career change, such size differences do not provide a definitive answer to the question for a number of reasons. For example, the two outcomes—leaving for academic reasons and career reasons—occur at different base rates in the population (twice as many people leave because of a career change as do for academic reasons). Because base rates can artificially attenuate observed relationships, if base rates differ, observed relationships should not be compared. Additionally, the attrition events in our analyses are not independent of one another (that is, if someone left for a career change, he or she did not leave for academic reasons, and vice versa). Moreover, the populations leaving for each reason are fundamentally different in any number of unmeasured ways.

A third notable difference is the relative size of the weights for the predictors in Model 2. In this case, the recommended weight for leadership composite is only slightly smaller in magnitude than that of the academic composite. In other words, relying solely on this set of analyses, we would suggest a noticeably different formula for selecting cadets than we would for the previous set of analyses.

Predicting USAFA GPA, MPA, and OPA

Table 5.3 shows the results for predicting GPA, MPA, and OPA, respectively. Similar to the results for graduation, when predicting GPA and OPA the direction of the relationship for selection panel score is again opposite what we would expect. For MPA, however, it is in the expected direction, and the relationship is statistically significant. For SAT, HS rank, academic composite, leadership composite, and selection composite, the relationships are again significant predictors in the direction expected, regardless of the outcome.

To further explore the impact of these issues on our conclusions, we conducted additional analyses comparing the prediction of the two outcomes. We first controlled for base rate differences in who dropped out for academic reasons ($N=954$) and who dropped out for career change reasons ($N=1,937$) by randomly selecting 500 observations from each group (graduates, nongraduates for academic reasons, and nongraduates for career change reasons). We then ran Models 1 through 3 for the graduates and nongraduates for academic reasons group and again for the graduates and nongraduates for career change reasons group. We did this 499 more times and summarized the distribution of standardized coefficients for each predictor in each model. This method produced similar results to what we found when running the regressions on the entire sample of individuals. Regression coefficients and the significance of the regression as a whole were noticeably larger for predicting leaving academic reasons than they were for predicting leaving for a career change. We also conducted a multivariate regression predicting all three outcomes simultaneously. The results again supported the same conclusion. Lastly, we compared the standard deviations on the predictor tests for the two groups that did not graduate. Standard deviations and means were similar, showing that range restriction differences across the groups could not account for the differences in magnitude of the regression coefficients.

Taken as a whole, these additional analyses provide further support for the conclusion that USAFA selection factors described above do a better job predicting who is likely to fail for academic reasons than they do at predicting who is likely to leave to pursue a different career.

Table 5.3
Predicting USAFA GPA, MPA, and OPA

	GPA (n = 20,364)			MPA (n = 12,972)			OPA (n = 20,790)		
	Model 1	Model 2	Model 3	Model 1	Model 2	Model 3	Model 1	Model 2	Model 3
R-squared	0.21	0.31	0.17	0.07	0.07	0.06	0.19	0.29	0.16
HS rank/size	−0.20*			−0.19*			−0.22*		
SAT composite	0.38*			0.12*			0.36*		
Academic composite		0.56*			0.25*			0.54*	
Leadership composite	0.09*	0.05*		0.13*	0.12*		0.10*	0.06*	
Selection panel score	0.01	−0.02*		0.02*	0.03*		0.01	−0.01*	
Selection composite			0.41*			0.25*			0.40*

NOTES: All regression models are significant at $p < 0.001$. Coefficients marked with an asterisk (*) are significant at $p < 0.05$. Results are reported in standardized units. For each predictor, the weight displayed indicates the average amount of change in the outcome that is associated with a one-standard-deviation change in the predictor. Standard errors for regression coefficients ranged from < 0.01 to 0.02.

Model 2 is again the best-fitting model for predicting OPA and GPA. It has noticeably (and statistically significantly) higher R-squared values for predicting GPA and OPA than Model 1. These findings hold even when selection panel score is removed from the model. For predicting MPA, however, Model 2 is not a significantly better predictor than the other models. It has only marginal improvement over Model 3.

Another interesting finding from Table 5.3 is that the overall magnitude of the R-squared values differs across the three USAFA outcomes. For predicting GPA and OPA, the R-squared values are quite large (R ranges from 0.40 to 0.56). In contrast, for predicting MPA, the R-squared values are more moderate in size (R ranges from 0.23 to 0.28). Overall, this suggests that USAFA admissions factors do a much better job in predicting GPA and OPA than they do in predicting MPA. Nevertheless, the R values for MPA are still of a large enough magnitude to conclude that the admissions factors are still useful in predicting MPA.

Like the results for graduation, Table 5.3 shows that we would make different recommendations for the ideal weights depending on which outcome is being predicted. For predicting MPA, Model 1 suggests that the optimal weight for HS rank is higher than the weight for SAT, and the leadership composite should optimally be weighted about the same as SAT. For predicting OPA and GPA, however, SAT receives the highest weight, nearly twice that of HS rank and more than three times that of the leadership composite. When looking at Model 2, the differences are even starker. Academic composite should be weighted twice that of leadership composite for predicting MPA, but nine times that of the leadership composite for predicting OPA and GPA.

Predicting Officer Career Outcomes

Below we examine validity for predicting promotions to major (O-4), lt. colonel (O-5), and colonel (O-6) for rated and nonrated officers. We first examine how well the admissions variables predict promotions, and then we examine how well USAFA outcomes predict promotions.

Predicting with the Admissions Variables

For promotion to grades O-4, O-5, and O-6, we used logistic regressions with the dependent variable as promoted (1) or not promoted (0). We limited the population of officers who are "not promoted" to only those who were eligible to see and also saw a promotions board but were not promoted. Anyone who separated from the Air Force before meeting a board was not considered in our analysis. In addition, anyone who was not a line officer or who was commissioned too recently to be eligible for promotion was excluded.[6] We present results separately for

---

[6]   Based on the overall rates of promotion in our data, we identified the following cutoffs for our analyses: 1990 for O-6, 1996 for O-5, and 1990 for O-4.

rated and nonrated line officers, as rates of promotion and factors leading to promotion can differ across those groups.[7]

As shown in Table 5.4, none of the admissions factors is significant for all three promotion grades. HS rank, academic composite, selection composite, and leadership composite are all significant for two grades, while SAT is only predictive of promotion to O-5. Once again, selection panel score is statistically significant in one case, but in the opposite direction of what would be expected.

Table 5.4
Predicting Rated Promotions from Admissions Variables

	Promotion to O-4 (n = 2,426)			Promotion to O-5 (n = 2,835)			Promotion to O-6 (n = 1,277)		
	Model 1	Model 2	Model 3	Model 1	Model 2	Model 3	Model 1	Model 2	Model 3
HS rank/size	−0.06*			−0.06*			0.00		
SAT composite	0.03			0.07*			0.04		
Academic composite		0.05*			0.14*			0.04	
Leadership composite	−0.03	−0.03		0.10*	0.10*		0.07*	0.07*	
Selection panel score	−0.03	−0.03		−0.07*	−0.07*		0.04	0.04	
Selection composite			−0.01			0.08*			0.08*

NOTES: All regression models are significant at $p < 0.001$. Coefficients marked with an asterisk (*) are significant at $p < 0.05$. Results are reported in standardized units. For each predictor, the weight displayed indicates the average amount of change in the outcome that is associated with a one-standard-deviation change in the predictor. Standard errors for regression coefficients ranged from 0.02 to 0.03.

[7]   We explored controlling for career field within both groups; however, in most cases the additions of the controls were not significant. Even in cases in which the controls were significant, the results for the rest of the predictors were remarkably similar, with very little difference in the AME and standardized coefficients in nearly all cases. Therefore, again for simplicity, we present the findings without controlling for career field. Cases where results differ meaningfully are noted as such.

Based on our measures of model fit (located in Appendix B), the best model for promotion to O-6 is Model 3 (the selection composite), the best model for promotion to O-5 is Model 2 (academic composite combined with leadership composite), and the best model for promotion to O-4 is inconclusive.

Like the rated results, findings for nonrated promotions (shown in Table 5.5) also differ depending on promotion level. This time, selection panel score is a significant predictor in the correct direction for predicting promotion to O-5; however, it is not a significant predictor of promotion to O-4 or O-6. Leadership composite and selection composite are also significant predictors of O-5. None of the admissions factors is a significant predictor of promotion to O-6, and leadership composite and academic composite are the only significant predictors of promotion to O-4.

Table 5.5
Predicting Nonrated Promotions from Admissions Variables

	Promotion to O-4 (n = 1,184)			Promotion to O-5 (n = 1,549)			Promotion to O-6 (n = 732)		
	Model 1	Model 2	Model 3	Model 1	Model 2	Model 3	Model 1	Model 2	Model 3
HS rank/size	−0.06			−0.02			0.00		
SAT composite	0.05			0.02			0.00		
Academic composite		0.10*			0.06			−0.01	
Leadership composite	0.08*	0.09*		0.13*	0.13*		0.04	0.04	
Selection panel score	0.00	0.00		0.11*	0.18*		−0.01	−0.01	
Selection composite			0.06			0.17*			0.00

NOTES: All regression models are significant at $p < 0.001$. Coefficients marked with an asterisk (*) are significant at $p < 0.05$. Results are reported in standardized units. For each predictor, the weight displayed indicates the average amount of change in the outcome that is associated with a one-standard-deviation change in the predictor. Standard errors for regression coefficients ranged from 0.02 to 0.05.

Predicting with USAFA Outcome Variables

In this section, we explored how well each of the USAFA outcome measures predicts promotion. Because all of the USAFA outcomes are generally regarded as important indicators of a cadet's potential as a future officer, it is worthwhile to explore the accuracy of that assumption. Moreover, better understanding how these more proximal measures of success at USAFA predict future success as officers can lead to additional recommendations for how to select cadets for entry into USAFA.

We again split the regression results into two groups: rated and nonrated line officers. The results of these analyses are presented in Tables 5.6 and 5.7. Comparing these tables to the results presented above, we found that the USAFA outcomes were much better predictors of promotions than were the USAFA admissions factors.

There are many explanations for this finding, including that USAFA has four more years to gather information on its cadets, much more information than it would have had at the time at which students applied to USAFA. The information is also more recent. That is, the time elapsed between admission to USAFA and promotion to major is at least four years longer than the time elapsed between graduation and promotion to major. Another explanation is that the information

Table 5.6
Predicting Rated Promotions from USAFA Outcomes

	Promotion to O-4 (n = 2,145)		Promotion to O-5 (n = 2,627)		Promotion to O-6 (n = 1,116)	
	Model 4	Model 5	Model 4	Model 5	Model 4	Model 5
Cumulative USAFA GPA	0.07*		0.16*		0.03	
Cumulative USAFA MPA	0.17*		0.21*		0.25*	
Cumulative USAFA OPA		0.18*		0.30*		0.20*

NOTES: All regression models are significant at $p < 0.001$. Coefficients marked with an asterisk (*) are significant at $p < 0.05$. Results are reported in standardized units. For each predictor, the weight displayed indicates the average amount of change in the outcome that is associated with a one-standard-deviation change in the predictor. Standard errors for regression coefficients ranged from 0.02 to 0.03.

Table 5.7
Predicting Nonrated Promotions from USAFA Outcomes

	Promotion to O-4 (n = 1,053)		Promotion to O-5 (n = 1,450)		Promotion to O-6 (n = 672)	
	Model 4	Model 5	Model 4	Model 5	Model 4	Model 5
Cumulative USAFA GPA	0.11*		0.15*		−0.06	
Cumulative USAFA MPA	0.11*		0.20*		0.23*	
Cumulative USAFA OPA		0.19*		0.28*		0.10*

NOTES: All regression models are significant at $p < 0.001$. Coefficients marked with an asterisk (*) are significant at $p < 0.05$. Results are reported in standardized units. For each predictor, the weight displayed indicates the average amount of change in the outcome that is associated with a one-standard-deviation change in the predictor. Standard errors for regression coefficients ranged from 0.03 to 0.05.

obtained on candidates is not as well standardized as that obtained while at USAFA. It is also the case that USAFA's standards for aptitude, physical fitness, and officer readiness are, at least theoretically, directly tailored to predict success as an officer. Differences in difficulty across high schools, differences in leniency bias across teachers providing student evaluation ratings, and differences in criteria used to select students for extracurricular activities are just some of the factors that can add irrelevant noise into the admissions selection variables. That noise then reduces their predictive validity.

Knowing that USAFA outcomes predict later promotions fairly well affirms that they are important outcomes when making selection decisions. In other words, if USAFA selects the students who are most likely to have good GPAs and MPA scores after four years at USAFA, it will also likely be selecting students who would have a greater potential to be promoted as officers years later. Interestingly, MPA is, overall, a slightly better predictor of promotions than GPA.

It is, however, also worth noting that USAFA outcomes are not the only determinants of later success in the Air Force. Many other factors can contribute to an officer's success, and USAFA outcomes should not be expected to be the sole predictor. Such factors as successful performance in particular career fields (such as rated career fields) can result in a higher likelihood of career success.

CHAPTER SIX

Recommendations

We recommend that Air Force and USAFA leadership consider three changes based on the results of this work. The first involves changes to the admissions formula based on the data analyses we could complete using the existing archival data sources. The last two involve collection and retention of information that was not available to us in this study but that would be ideal to have available for future research efforts.

Adjust the Selection Composite Formula

The management of the selection panel, the scoring, and the weighting of the scores are all policy levers that can be used to shape admissions to better achieve desired outcomes at USAFA and in the Air Force. The selection algorithm, therefore, can and should be adjusted to best achieve these objectives. From our examination of USAFA student data and officer promotions data, we found evidence that supports the use of the current selection composite; however, we also found evidence that that the formula for this measure could be improved.

First, we saw repeated evidence that the use of the selection panel score in the selection composite was not helping to select the best candidates; in fact, it was hindering it. In all cases, eliminating selection panel score from the regression formula did not harm predictive validity, and, in many cases, removing it resulted in a statistically significant improvement in prediction. Thus, its continued use as a compensatory element in the selection composite (higher selection panel scores compensate for lower scores on the leadership or academic composites) is not supported in our data. Based on this, we recommend removing the selection panel score from the selection composite formula. Although we recommend removing it from the formula, we acknowledge that a selection panel score in some form could still be retained as a selection factor, if its purpose and usefulness can be justified on other grounds.[1]

Second, we saw evidence suggesting that the weighting of the remaining two elements in the formula could be improved. As shown in the regression analyses, recommended weights vary widely depending on the outcome to be predicted. Given those differences, we recommend considering a combined set of weights that takes into consideration the multiple outcomes. Although there are many possible combined solutions for the weights that could be justified, based on the entirety of the regression results, we see reasonable justification for a conceptual weight of around 75 percent for the academic composite and around 25 percent for the leadership composite (with a weight of zero for the selection panel score, per our recommendation above). If such a formula were to be implemented, it would be a notable change from the composition of the existing admissions formula (60 percent academic composite, 20 percent leadership composite, and 20 percent selection panel score). For more discussion on how we arrived at these estimated proportions and how to convert them to a raw score formula, see Appendixes C and B, respectively.

---

[1]   Although the data show that removing the existing selection panel score from the formula would improve prediction, it might be possible to introduce a new selection panel score into the formula if the results of the selection panel could be meaningfully improved (such as by including greater structure in the process or changing the information considered by the panel). However, validation evidence to support an improved selection panel would be needed. In addition, we cannot conclude that the selection panel information should be eliminated entirely from the selection process, given the present data. It is very possible that some applicants were denied admission to USAFA because of their selection panel score, and those rejection decisions might have been accurate at predicting who would not succeed. Those people would not be present in our data because they were never selected; thus, we can neither confirm nor deny that possibility with our data. If people are being correctly rejected on the basis of selection panel score, USAFA may want to consider using the selection panel score solely to screen out people that the selection panel identifies as problematic. However, because the validity of selection panel score for use as a screening-out tool has not been confirmed, a closer examination of its validity for that use would be needed.

Regardless of which results USAFA chooses to focus on, it is worth noting that no single result should be considered at the exclusion of all of the other findings. In all regressions predicting the more proximal outcomes of USAFA success, the best-fitting model placed a noticeably higher weight on academic composite, even when predicting MPA, and both MPA and GPA are good predictors of later promotions. Although a few of the promotions results suggested a higher weight for leadership composite, that finding was not consistent across all grades of promotions, nor was it consistent across the rated and non-rated populations. For that reason, we would not recommend that the weight for the leadership composite exceed that of the academic composite. And we see sound justification for continuing to place a much larger weight (at least double the weight) on the academic composite relative to the leadership composite.

Lastly, it is worth noting that although it may be straightforward to discuss the formula using percentages, the final formula itself would need to be transformed back into unstandardized units in order to be applied to actual applicant scores. This transformation is explained in Appendix B.

Collect Additional Information on Applicants

We recommend that USAFA consider collecting new information on its applicants. A wide variety of measures have been identified as useful tools for predicting performance in a wide variety of workplace and managerial settings. It would therefore be useful to explore whether any of these measures could add value to the USAFA selection process as well. Examples of measures that could be explored include personality tests, situational judgment tests, critical thinking performance tasks, and writing tests. All of these have shown promise, and their usefulness, cost-effectiveness, and difficulty to fake have improved as technology has improved. In some cases, these types of measures can tap content domains and individual difference characteristics that are entirely different from the academic domains captured in traditional standardized tests, such as the SAT. As a result, they are often used to predict nonacademic performance areas, such as teamwork or leadership. We recommend collecting data using some of these measures experimentally now and retaining those data in archival data files. The predictive validity of these measures can be examined in several years once outcome data (such as graduation or USAFA GPA and MPA) are available. If those tests prove useful additions to the academic and leadership composites, we would recommend including them in USAFA's selection process.

Improve Data Retention and Maintenance

We strongly recommend that studies examining predictive validity be undertaken periodically to verify that a selection system is working as intended. We also recommend that as much available data on applicants as possible be included in that predictive validation study to help determine whether improvements to the formula can be made by including different information. However, to do so requires a rich and complete source of longitudinal data that is well documented and maintained over time. Although the final selection algorithm scores have been fairly well maintained, other useful information on applicants collected at the time at which they applied has not been consistently retained (e.g., high school course and GPA information). This severely limited what we could examine and recommend in this study.

As a result, another main finding of our study is that there is a need for increased data retention and better maintenance of USAFA's archival data sources. Conducting a predictive validation study is the ideal approach to validating a selection system. However, doing so requires that data be retained on all applicants and all selectees at an institution. That data should contain scores on all possible measures taken at the time of application to the institution and should track their performance over time. In this study, we examined prediction of promotions that occurred decades after people had been selected into the institution. As a result, the data we relied on was decades old. If the Air Force hopes to conduct such a study again, it should ensure that the data being collected and retained today are maintained in such a way that they meet the needs of researchers in the future.

Among the recommendations we would make for improving data retention and maintenance is establishing a central location in the Air Force responsible for storing and maintaining data on USAFA applicants, cadets, and officers. That data could be collected from USAFA annually. Currently, the Air Force Personnel Center stores and maintains a variety of archival data sets on its military and civilian personnel. Data on USAFA's applicants and cadets could be added to its area of responsibility. Data code books explaining each data element should be produced annually, and the data should be examined closely to ensure that the information is consistent with the codes and explanations provided in the code book. As we discovered in our exploration of the data, there were many codes in the data that were unexplained. For example, for several years HS GPA ranged from 0.00 to 10.00; however, no explanation for how to interpret a GPA higher than a 5.00 is available. These types of data quality issues should be identified and corrected or explained in detail in the code books annually.

Recommendations for new data elements to include should be made annually as well. We discovered that although many elements are collected on individuals to calculate the composite scores, in many cases, only the overall composite score was retained in the data. Similarly, records of SAT scores in some years contained only total SAT scores rather than SAT subtest scores. Although the total scores may be what is ultimately used in making the selection decisions, a failure to retain the details on these other elements means that we cannot explore whether we could recommend improving the existing composite scores. For that reason, we suggest that USAFA maintain records on all elements considered in the selection process. That includes, for example, any ratings that the selection panel assigns to letters of recommendation or written personal statements. If such ratings assigned by the selection panel were available, we could possibly suggest ways to redesign the selection panel scoring process to make the selection panel scores more useful in predicting the outcomes we explored here.[2]

Although we are recommending that these data be retained and maintained, we note that recent USAFA data are much better maintained than the older data. Much of the information we would recommend for retention is now being retained. In time, those data will mature, and they could be further mined for predicting the outcomes we described here. We therefore recommend that data retention and maintenance on the admissions factors and USAFA outcomes continue to be carefully attended to in the years going forward.

We also would recommend that the Air Force consider developing a method for capturing systematic performance evaluations on its officers at various points in their careers for research purposes only. This would eliminate the current concerns that performance ratings have too little variance for use in predictive validation studies. Collecting this type of data would be beneficial in many aspects of personnel research efforts. For example, it could be used to improve promotions board processes, identify training needs, improve classification decisions, and define the main elements of leadership and officer performance. In addition, if such evaluations of performance could be collected on officers in their second year of service, in as few as six years we could begin to explore the predictive validity of the admissions factors that are collected on applicants to USAFA today.

---

[2]   One of the main factors considered by the selection panel is the ALO's ratings of the candidate; however, those ratings tend to show little variance across candidates.

Average Marginal Effects, Unstandardized Beta Coefficients, and Fit Indexes

Tables A.1 through A.7 provide additional regression output for all of the models discussed in the main body of this report.

For all logistic regressions (Tables A.1 and A.3 through A.7), we report the marginal effect for each observation in the regression and average these to obtain the average marginal effect (AME). For the linear regressions (Table A.2), we report unstandardized beta weights.

For the logit model, a marginal effect can be interpreted as the percentage point change in the probability of the outcome in response to a one-unit change in the value of the independent variable (all else constant). To illustrate the interpretation of the AME, in Table A.6, Model 4 shows an AME of 0.0565 for cumulative USAFA GPA predicting promotion to O-4. The model therefore predicts that, on average, as a person's GPA increases by 1 point, his or her probability of being promoted to O-4 increases by 5.65 percentage points.

Note that AME magnitude differences between predictors in the same regression are meaningless. Because the scale for each of the predictors differs, and many have a range of more than 1,000 points (e.g., SAT scores range from 400 to 1600), the practical significance of a 1-point change can vary drastically from predictor to predictor. For example, a 1-point change in USAFA GPA (say, from a 2.8 GPA to a 3.8 GPA) is a large jump and, therefore, would be expected to have a large impact on the outcome being predicted. In contrast, a 1-point change in SAT scores (say, from a 1200 to a 1201) would be considered to have a negligible impact on scores. This is why the AMEs below appear small, yet they are still significant. This difference in scale across predictors is not a concern when examining the standardized coefficients shown in the output provided in the main body of the report. Because the scale for several of the predictors in Tables A.1 through A.5 is quite large (e.g., SAT scores range from 400 to 1600), the AMEs appear to be quite small (< 0.0001), even though they are still significant.

Table A.1
AME and Fit Indexes for Predicting Graduation (Academic)

	Graduation (Academic)				Graduation (Career Change)			
	Model 1	Model 2	Model 3	Recommended Model	Model 1	Model 2	Model 3	Recommended Model
N	22,375	22,375	22,375	22,375	23,358	23,358	23,358	23,358
−2ln(L)	7,554	7,237	7,699	7,275	13,196	13,150	13,345	13,257
AIC	7,564	7,245	7,703	7,281	13,206	13,158	13,349	13,263
BIC	7,604	7,277	7,719	7,305	13,247	13,190	13,365	13,287
HS rank	−0.0754*				0.0190			
SAT composite	0.0002*				0.0001*			
Academic composite		0.0001*		0.0001*		<0.0001*		0.0001*
Leadership composite	<0.0001*	<0.0001*		<0.0001*	0.0001*	0.0001*		0.0000
Selection panel score	−0.0001*	−0.0001*			−0.0002*	−0.0002*		
Selection composite			0.0003*				0.0001*	

NOTES: −2ln(L) = −2 multiplied by the log of the maximum value of the likelihood function. Chi-squared for all models is significant at $p < 0.0001$. Asterisk (*) denotes a significant coefficient in the logistic regression ($p < 0.05$).

Table A.2
Unstandardized Beta Coefficients for Predicting USAFA GPA, MPA, and OPA

	USAFA GPA				USAFA MPA				USAFA OPA			
	Model 1	Model 2	Model 3	Recommended Model	Model 2	Model 3	Model 5	Recommended Model	Model 2	Model 3	Model 5	Recommended Model
R-squared	0.208	0.311	0.165	0.311	0.071	0.075	0.061	0.075	0.198	0.290	0.162	0.290
HS rank/size	−0.858*				−0.698*				−0.764*			
SAT composite	0.002*				<0.001*				0.001*			
Academic composite		0.001*		0.0009*		<0.001*		0.0003*				0.0007*
Leadership composite	<0.001*	<0.001*		0.0001*	<0.001*	<0.001*		0.0002*	<0.001*	<0.001*		0.0001*
Selection panel score	0.000	<0.001*		<0.001*	<0.001*	<0.001*		0.000	0.000	<0.001*		
Selection composite			0.003*				0.002*				0.003*	
Constant	0.325*	−0.028	0.339*	−0.053	2.109*	1.737*	1.718*	1.7999*	0.812*	0.463*	0.748*	0.4462*

NOTES: GPA n = 20,364; MPA n = 12,972; OPA n = 20,790. Coefficients marked with an asterisk (*) are significant at $p < 0.05$. For MPA, the marginal improvement shown by Models 2, 3, and 5 is likely a statistical artifact of including more predictors and does not reflect any real improvement in prediction. Small improvements resulting from the addition of predictors are usually due to chance errors in the data leading to the illusion of an improved model (Hawkins, 2004). This is one example of overfitting.

Table A.3
AME and Fit Indexes for Predicting Rated Promotions Using Admissions Criteria

	Promotion to O-4 (n = 2,426)			Promotion to O-5 (n = 2,835)			Promotion to O-6 (n = 1,277)		
	Model 2	Model 3	Model 5	Model 2	Model 3	Model 5	Model 2	Model 3	Model 5
Chi-squared p-value	0.011	0.030	0.609	0.000	0.000	0.001	0.102	0.058	0.013
−2ln(L)	2,821	2,825	2,834	3,015	3,004	3,045	1,735	1,735	1,736
AIC	2,831	2,833	2,838	3,025	3,012	3,049	1,745	1,743	1,740
BIC	2,860	2,856	2,849	3,055	3,035	3,061	1,770	1,763	1,750
HS rank/size	−0.3379*			−0.3044*			0.0103		
SAT composite	0.0001			0.0003*			0.0002		
Academic composite		0.0001*			0.0002*			0.0001	
Leadership composite	−0.0001	−0.0001		0.0002*	0.0002*		0.0002*	0.0002*	
Selection panel score	−0.0001	−0.0001		−0.0001*	−0.0001*		0.0001	0.0001	
Selection composite			−0.0001			0.0004*			0.0006*

NOTES: −2ln(L) = −2 multiplied by the log of the maximum value of the likelihood function. Asterisk (*) denotes a significant coefficient in the logistic regression (p < 0.05).

Table A.4
AME and Fit Indexes for Models Predicting Nonrated Promotions Using Admissions Criteria

	Promotion to O-4			Promotion to O-5			Promotion to O-6		
	Model 1	Model 2	Model 3	Model 1	Model 2	Model 3	Model 1	Model 2	Model 3
N	1,184	1,184	1,184	1,549	1,549	1,549	732	732	732
Chi-squared p-value	0.057	0.014	0.086	0.000	0.000	0.000	0.912	0.800	0.993
–2ln(L)	1,267	1,266	1,273	1,519	1,517	1,524	1,001	1,001	1,002
AIC	1,277	1,274	1,277	1,529	1,525	1,528	1,011	1,009	1,006
BIC	1,302	1,294	1,287	1,556	1,547	1,539	1,034	1,027	1,015
HS rank/size	–0.2839			–0.0875			0.0052		
SAT composite	0.0002			0.0001			0.0000		
Academic composite		0.0001*			0.0001			0.0000	
Leadership composite	0.0002*	0.0002*		0.0002*	0.0002*		0.0001	0.0001	
Selection panel score	0.0000	0.0000		0.0002*	0.0002*		0.0000	0.0000	
Selection composite			0.0003			0.0008*			0.0000

NOTES: –2ln(L) = –2 multiplied by the log of the maximum value of the likelihood function. Asterisk (*) denotes a significant coefficient in the logistic regression ($p < 0.05$).

Table A.5
AME and Fit Indexes for Models Using Academic and Leadership Composites Only for Predicting Promotions

	Nonrated			Rated		
	Promoted to O-4	Promoted to O-5	Promoted to O-6	Promoted to O-4	Promoted to O-5	Promoted to O-6
N	1,184	1,549	732	2,426	2,835	1,277
Chi-squared p-value	0.005	0.000	0.629	0.025	0.000	0.045
$-2\ln(L)$	1,266	1,528	1,001	2,827	3,011	1,736
AIC	1,272	1,534	1,007	2,833	3,017	1,742
BIC	1,287	1,551	1,020	2,850	3,035	1,757
Academic composite	0.0001*	0.0001	0.000	0.0001*	0.0002*	0.0001
Leadership composite	0.0002*	0.0002*	0.000	-0.0001	0.0002*	0.0002*

NOTES: $-2\ln(L) = -2$ multiplied by the log of the maximum value of the likelihood function. Asterisk (*) denotes a significant coefficient in the logistic regression ($p < 0.05$).

Table A.6
AME and Fit Indexes for Predicting Rated Promotions Using USAFA Outcomes

	Promotion to O-4		Promotion to O-5		Promotion to O-6	
	Model 4	Model 5	Model 4	Model 5	Model 4	Model 5
N	2,145	2,145	2,627	2,627	1,116	1,116
−2ln(L)	2,445	2,465	2,697	2,721	1,456	1,487
AIC	2,451	2,469	2,703	2,725	1,462	1,491
BIC	2,468	2,480	2,721	2,737	1,478	1,501
Cumulative GPA USAFA	0.0565*		0.1173*		0.0316	
Cumulative MPA USAFA	0.2184*		0.2476*		0.3935*	
Cumulative OPA USAFA		0.1669*		0.2592*		0.2234*

NOTES: −2ln(L) = −2 multiplied by the log of the maximum value of the likelihood function. Chi-squared for all models is significant at $p < 0.0001$. Asterisk (*) denotes a significant coefficient in the logistic regression ($p < 0.05$).

Table A.7
AME and Fit Indexes for Predicting Nonrated Promotions Using USAFA Outcomes

	Promotion to O-4		Promotion to O-5		Promotion to O-6	
	Model 4	Model 5	Model 4	Model 5	Model 4	Model 5
N	1,053	1,053	1,450	1,450	672	672
Chi-squared p-value	0.000	0.000	0.000	0.000	0.000	0.026
–2ln(L)	1,105	1,106	1,339	1,349	896	914
AIC	1,111	1,110	1,345	1,353	902	918
BIC	1,126	1,120	1,361	1,363	915	927
Cumulative GPA USAFA	0.0750*		0.0881*		–0.0524	
Cumulative MPA USAFA	0.1281*		0.2041*		0.3609*	
Cumulative OPA USAFA		0.1510*		0.1995*		0.1042*

NOTES: –2ln(L) = –2 multiplied by the log of the maximum value of the likelihood function. Asterisk (*) denotes a significant coefficient in the logistic regression ($p < 0.05$).

Means and Standard Deviations for Each Analysis Population

This appendix reports means and standard deviations (SDs) for each of the populations examined in the regressions reported in the main body of the report (see Tables B.1 and B.2). This information can be used to convert any of the standardized coefficients reported in the main body of the report for use as a new selection formula. To do so requires applying a linear transformation to each standardized coefficient (β_j) included in the regression equation as follows:

$$\textit{Selection Score} = [\beta_1 * (X_{1i} - \textit{Mean}_1) / SD_1] + [\beta_2 * (X_{2i} - \textit{Mean}_2) / SD_2]$$
$$+ \dots [\beta_j * (X_{ji} - \textit{Mean}_j) / SD_j],$$

where *Selection Score* represents the final score that would be assigned to a candidate, j represents the total number of predictors in the regression equation, β represents the unstandardized weight associated with a given predictor in the regression equation, X_i represents a candidate's raw score on the predictor, and *Mean$_j$* and *SD$_j$* represent the means and SDs for the corresponding predictor and outcome reported in the tables below.[1]

If the desired formula is defined by percentages that total to 100 instead of standardized beta weights (an option discussed in Chapter Six), the formula could be adjusted as follows:

---

[1]   Note that in the formula above, we have assumed that there will not be meaningful differences in the distribution of scores in the outcome measures in future populations.

$$Selection\ Score = [\%_1 * (X_{1i} - Mean_1) / SD_1] + [\%_2 * (X_{2i} - Mean_2) / SD_2] + \dots [\%_j * (X_{ji} - Mean_j) / SD_j],$$

where % indicates the percentage assigned in the formula, and all other variables are the same as defined above.

Table B.1
USAFA Outcome Analyses Means and SDs

	Graduated Versus Academic Dropout		Graduated Versus Career Goal Change Reason Dropout		Cumulative USAFA GPA		Cumulative USAFA MPA		Cumulative USAFA OPA	
	Mean	SD	Mean	SD	Mean	SD	Mean	SD	Mean	SD
Cumulative USAFA GPA					2.96	0.45	2.91	0.28	2.93	0.37
HS rank/size	0.08	0.11	0.08	0.11	0.08	0.11	0.07	0.08	0.08	0.11
SAT composite	1301.11	95.99	1302.17	96.07	1305.09	95.02	1308.48	93.33	1304.67	95.33
Academic composite	3207.90	289.15	3211.75	287.25	3225.76	283.22	3206.12	279.95	3227.89	283.68
Leadership composite	1710.57	194.52	1707.41	194.31	1711.83	194.21	1703.46	195.00	1717.53	192.71
Selection panel score	572.11	111.72	572.60	110.44	570.37	113.52	582.85	77.72	570.71	112.49
Selection composite	794.51	54.35	795.15	54.20	795.85	54.64	793.94	47.65	795.80	54.48

Table B.2
Promotion Outcome Analyses Means and SDs

	Promoted to O-4				Promoted to O-5				Promoted to O-6			
	Nonrated		Rated		Nonrated		Rated		Nonrated		Rated	
	Mean	SD	Mean	SD	Mean	SD	Mean	SD	Mean	SD	Mean	SD
HS rank/size	0.06	0.08	0.06	0.08	0.06	0.08	0.06	0.07	0.06	0.08	0.06	0.07
SAT composite	1299.70	100.95	1304.28	91.16	1315.14	97.76	1317.82	91.16	1306.72	104.25	1310.16	91.25
Academic composite	3155.66	279.96	3150.41	262.08	3215.53	286.54	3204.33	274.03	3184.74	287.00	3173.73	266.75
Leadership composite	1585.79	170.25	1609.65	166.22	1654.74	195.07	1666.54	186.45	1601.38	169.22	1611.05	162.43
Selection panel score	531.23	194.50	521.03	184.56	554.49	149.89	546.01	146.75	546.92	173.19	509.81	184.26
Selection composite	763.69	58.76	762.34	58.02	785.21	58.51	782.15	58.63	773.24	57.71	762.91	61.15
Cumulative USAFA GPA	2.85	0.48	2.90	0.47	2.89	0.46	2.95	0.45	2.91	0.48	2.98	0.47
Cumulative USAFA MPA	2.88	0.28	2.95	0.28	2.91	0.28	2.98	0.28	2.93	0.28	3.01	0.28
Cumulative USAFA OPA	2.85	0.40	2.91	0.38	2.90	0.38	2.96	0.37	2.91	0.40	2.99	0.39

Estimating New Recommended Formula Weights

To help estimate the ideal weights for a formula using just academic and leadership composite, we reran all analyses using only those two predictors. The standardized regression results are shown in Table C.1, and Table C.2 displays the same results transformed into percentages totaling to 100.[1]

There are many ways to combine the information presented in these tables into a single recommended admissions formula; thus, a variety of weights could be justified. Taking into consideration some or all of the equations in Table C.2, one could argue for weights ranging from 65 percent to 85 percent for the academic composite and 15 percent to 35 percent for the leadership composite.

Certain outcomes could certainly be argued to be more important than others, and greater emphasis could be placed on those regression results. For example, because we know that MPA is a good predictor of later promotions, USAFA could choose to place greater emphasis on the formula for predicting MPA than on the formulas for the other USAFA outcomes. In this example, there could be justification for a formula in which the academic composite would have about twice the

---

[1] To illustrate this transformation, consider just the MPA regression information. The column for MPA shows the standardized coefficients for both predictors. The academic composite coefficient is 0.24, and the leadership composite coefficient is 0.12. To convert those two coefficients into percentages, we would divide each by the sum of both coefficients and multiply by 100. This would result in a weight of 67 percent for the academic composite score [0.24 / (0.12 + 0.24) * 100 = 67 percent] and 33 percent for the leadership composite [0.12 / (0.12 + 0.24) * 100 = 33 percent]. We applied this transformation to each of the regression results in Table C.1 to produce the information in Table C.2.

Table C.1
Regression Coefficients for a Model That Includes Only Academic and Leadership Composites

Variables	Graduation Versus Academic Failure	Graduation Versus Career Change	GPA	MPA	OPA	Promotions Nonrated			Promotions Rated		
						O-4	O-5	O-6	O-4	O-5	O-6
N	22,375	23,358	20,364	12,972	20,790	1,184	1,549	732	2,426	2,835	1,277
R-squared			0.31	0.08	0.29						
Academic composite	0.42*	0.11*	0.55*	0.24*	0.53*	0.10*	0.05	-0.01	0.06*	0.14*	0.04
Leadership composite	0.07*	0.06*	0.04*	0.12*	0.06*	0.09*	0.15*	0.04	-0.03	0.09*	0.07*

NOTES: All models above are significant at $p < 0.05$, except for the model for rated promotions to O-6. Coefficients marked with an asterisk (*) are significant at $p < 0.05$. Results are reported in standardized units. For each predictor, the weight displayed indicates the average amount of change in the outcome that is associated with a one-standard-deviation change in the predictor. Standard errors for regression coefficients ranged from 0.01 to 0.04.

Table C.2
Regression Formulas Expressed as Percentages Totaling to 100

Variables	Graduation Versus Academic Failure	Graduation Versus Career Change	GPA	MPA	OPA	Promotions Nonrated			Promotions Rated		
						O-4	O-5	O-6	O-4	O-5	O-6
Academic composite	86%	65%	93%	67%	90%	53%	—	—	100%	61%	—
Leadership composite	14%	35%	7%	33%	10%	47%	100%	100%	—	39%	100%
Total	100%	100%	100%	100%	100%	100%	100%	100%	100%	100%	100%

NOTE: In cases in which the regression suggested negative weights or the weights were not significantly different from zero, we did not assign a percentage.

weight of the leadership composite (i.e., 67 percent and 33 percent, respectively).

Nevertheless, combining information across regression formulas would be the best approach. Given that MPA is, overall, a slightly better predictor of promotions than GPA, this suggests that while both GPA and MPA are important, focusing on finding the admissions factors that predict GPA, for example, at the expense of predicting MPA may not be the best approach. Knowing that the equations for predicting MPA favor a larger weight for the leadership composite than the equations for predicting GPA, and that MPA is at least equally as important as GPA for predicting later promotions, we would suggest considering a selection equation that takes both results into consideration. Similarly, the graduation outcomes should be included as well, as graduation is by definition a requirement for commissioning as an officer. If students do not graduate, they will not become officers and will not be considered for promotion. Thus, a set of weights that takes all of those results into consideration would fall around 75 percent for the academic composite and 25 percent for the leadership composite.

Regardless of which equations are combined, we caution readers against averaging across any of the formulas in Table C.1 without first transforming the data. First, note that an average of Table C.2 does not produce the same recommended weights as an average of Table C.1. Moreover, because the populations for each regression differed (some are range restricted because they included only those who graduated, for example) and the strength of the overall regression relationship varied depending on the outcome to be predicted, a simple average of the weights in Table C.1 does not capture a true average of the relative impact of each variable. Instead, to average the coefficients, they should first be transformed back into the original applicable unstandardized units and then averaged. For each equation shown in Table C.1, standardized weights can be transformed into the unstandardized units using the means and SDs provided in Appendix B for each relevant population. The resulting unstandardized weights for each predictor could then be averaged across all of the equations to produce a single set of unstandardized weights. Those could then be transformed back into percentages (summing to 100) for ease of interpretation.

References

American Educational Research Association, American Psychological Association, National Council on Measurement in Education, and Joint Committee on Standards for Educational and Psychological Testing, *Standards for Educational and Psychological Testing*, 2014.

Brogden, Hubert E., and Erwin K. Taylor, "The Theory and Classification of Criterion Bias," *Educational and Psychological Measurement*, 1950.

Butler, Richard P., and Clark McCauley, "Extraordinary Stability and Ordinary Predictability of Academic Success at the United States Military Academy," *Journal of Educational Psychology*, Vol. 79, No. 1, 1987, p. 83.

College Board, "SAT I Individual Score Equivalents," 2015a. As of November 12, 2015:
http://research.collegeboard.org/programs/sat/data/equivalence/sat-individual

———, "SAT-ACT Concordance Tables," 2015b. As of November 12, 2015:
http://research.collegeboard.org/programs/sat/data/concordance

Copas, J. B., "Regression, Prediction and Shrinkage," *Journal of the Royal Statistical Society*, Series B (Methodological), Vol. 45, No. 3, 1983, pp. 311–354.

Dempsey, Jack R., and Jonathan C. Fast, "Predicting Attrition: An Empirical Study at the United States Air Force Academy," 1976.

Didier, Jeremy, "Evaluating Cadet Leadership Positions at the U.S. Air Force USAFA," Santa Monica, Calif.: RAND Corporation, RGSD-307, 2012. As of November 12, 2015:
http://www.rand.org/pubs/rgs_dissertations/RGSD307.html

Geiser, Saul, and Maria Veronica Santelices, "Validity of High-School Grades in Predicting Student Success Beyond the Freshman Year: High-School Record vs. Standardized Tests as Indicators of Four-Year College Outcomes," *Research & Occasional Paper Series*, CSHE, 6.07, Center for Studies in Higher Education, 2007.

Hanser, Lawrence M., and Mustafa Oguz, *United States Service Academy Admissions: Selecting for Success at the Military Academy/West Point and as an Officer*, Santa Monica, Calif.: RAND Corporation, RR-723-OSD, 2015. As of November 12, 2015:
http://www.rand.org/pubs/research_reports/RR723.html

Hawkins, Douglas M., "The Problem of Overfitting," *Journal of Chemical Information Computer Science*, Vol. 44, 2004, pp. 1–12.

Joint Committee on Standards for Educational and Psychological Testing, *Standards for Educational and Psychological Testing*, Washington, D.C.: American Educational Research Association, 1999.

Kulatunga Moruzi, Chan, and Geoffrey R. Norman, "Validity of Admissions Measures in Predicting Performance Outcomes: The Contribution of Cognitive and Non-Cognitive Dimensions," *Teaching and Learning in Medicine*, Vol. 14, No. 1, 2002, pp. 34–42.

Lievens, Filip, Tine Buyse, and Paul R. Sackett, "The Operational Validity of a Video-Based Situational Judgment Test for Medical College Admissions: Illustrating the Importance of Matching Predictor and Criterion Construct Domains," *Journal of Applied Psychology*, Vol. 90, No. 3, 2005, p. 442.

Miller, Robert E., *Predicting First Year Achievement of Air Force Academy Cadets*, Class of 1964, No. PRL-TDR-64-18, Personnel Research Lab, Lackland AFB, Tex., 1964.

Sackett, Paul R., and Hyuckseung Yang, "Correction for Range Restriction: An Expanded Typology," *Journal of Applied Psychology*, Vol. 85, No. 1, 2000, p. 112.

Society for Industrial and Organizational Psychology, Inc., *Principles for the Validation and Use of Personnel Selection Procedures*, 4th ed., Bowling Green, Ohio, 2003. As of November 12, 2015:
http://www.siop.org/_principles/principles.pdf

United States Air Force, *Air Force IMT 2030*, USAF Drug and Alcohol Abuse Certificate Washington, D.C.: Department of the Air Force, 1999. As of November 12, 2015:
https://admissions.usafa.edu/RRS/AF_Form_2030.pdf

———, *Admissions Liaison Officer Handbook*, Washington, D.C.: Department of the Air Force, 2010. As of November 12, 2015:
http://southtexasalo.org/External%20Files/ALO%20Handbook.pdf

United States Air Force Academy, Selection Panel Training Briefing for the USAFA class of 2015, undated.

————, *Form 146, Air Force Academy Candidate Personal Data Record*, Washington, D.C.: Department of the Air Force, 2003a. As of November 12, 2015:
http://www.reginfo.gov/public/do/DownloadDocument?objectID=3762601

United States Air Force Academy, *Form 147, U.S. Air Force Academy Candidate Activities Record*, Washington, D.C.: Department of the Air Force, 2003b. As of November 12, 2015:
http://www.reginfo.gov/public/do/
PRAViewIC?ref_nbr=200707-0701-001&icID=5070

————, *Form 145, U.S. Air Force Academy School Official's Evaluation of Candidate*, Washington, D.C.: Department of the Air Force, 2006a. As of November 12, 2015:
https://admissions.usafa.edu/secure/Online/Forms/Form145.pdf

————, *Form O-158, USAF Academy Candidate Fitness Assessment Exam Score Sheet*, Washington, D.C.: Department of the Air Force, 2006b. As of November 12, 2015:
https://aloweb.usafa.edu/Forms/CFA.pdf

————, *Form 148, Air Force Academy Request for Secondary School Transcript*, Washington, D.C.: Department of the Air Force, 2007. As of November 12, 2015:
http://www.reginfo.gov/public/do/DownloadDocument?objectID=15701601

————, *Demographic Profile of the Class of 2012*, Colorado Springs, Colo.: United States Air Force Academy, 2008. As of November 12, 2015:
https://admissions.usafa.edu/RRC/Profile_Class2012(11Jul08).pdf

————, *Demographic Profile of the Class of 2013*, Colorado Springs, Colo.: United States Air Force Academy, 2009. As of November 12, 2015:
https://admissions.usafa.edu/RRC/Class_of_2013_profile.pdf

————, *Demographic Profile of the Class of 2014*, Colorado Springs, Colo.: United States Air Force Academy, 2010a. As of November 12, 2015:
http://paulryan.house.gov/uploadedfiles/usafa_2014.pdf

————, *Instructions to Candidates*, Colorado Springs, Colo.: United States Air Force Academy, 2010b. As of November 12, 2015:
https://admissions.usafa.edu/secure/online/WebPCQ2015.pdf

————, "The Application Process," 2012. As of November 12, 2015:
http://www.academyadmissions.com/admissions/the-application-process/application-steps/

USAFA—*see* United States Air Force Academy.

USAFA, Association of Graduates, *Parent Handbook 2012/2013*, 2012. Accessed on November 12, 2015:
http://www.usafa.org/Documents/Connect/ParentHandbook2012-13.pdf

Valentine, Lonnie D., *Air Force Academy Selection Variables as Predictors of Success in Pilot Training*, AD 263982, Aeronautical Systems Division, Wright-Patterson Air Force Base, Ohio, September 1961.